GW01048638

the
SECURE ONLINE
BUSINESS

Is your content secure from prying eyes?

...yes of course, it's signed and sealed in an envelope. But we don't send letters in envelopes these days, it's all email. So why don't we secure our email's like we do our letters?

With XenoMail you can - and it's as easy as using an envelope.

XenoMail is integrated into Microsoft Outlook and other email packages, it appears as an additional button on your toolbar, so it's simple to use.

Why not try XenoMail today, visit www.indiciisalus.com for your free 60 day trial.

Secure Email with XenoMail™

Certified Secure

XenoMail by indicii salus

indicii salus
Securing the Internet. Enabling trust.™

the
SECURE ONLINE BUSINESS

e-commerce, IT functionality & business continuity

consultant editor **adam jolly**

First published in Great Britain and the United States in 2003 by Kogan Page Limited

120 Pentonville Road
London N1 9JN
www.kogan-page.co.uk

22883 Quicksilver Drive
Sterling VA 20166–2012
USA

British Library Cataloguing-in-Publication Data

A CIP record for this book is available from the British Library

ISBN 0 7494 3936 X

Typeset by Saxon Graphics Ltd, Derby.
Printed and bound in Great Britain by Cambrian Printers Ltd, Aberystwyth

Contents

Foreword   xiii
George Cox, Director General, Institute of Directors

Introduction
Adam Jolly   *xv*

Part 1: Information at risk

1.1   The business case for information security   3
      Nick Coleman, Head of Security Services, IBM and Chairman, SAINT
1.2   The demand for continuous information   12
      Rick Cudworth, Partner, KPMG LLP
1.3   The threat from cybercrime   18
      The Fraud Advisory Panel, Cybercrime Working Group, ICAEW
1.4   Recent attack trends   22
      Stuart Eaton, Centrinet
1.5   Recognising the enemy within   26
      Declan Grogan, Security Designers
1.6   Cyberliabilities in the workplace   33
      Richard Woudberg, Legal Counsel, Integralis
1.7   Data complacency   37
      Humphrey Browning, Head of Technical Consultancy, Nexor
1.8   The marketing dimension   41
      Michael Harrison, Chairman, Harrison Smith Associates

      Stamping out the bugs   47
      Tony Neate, Industry Liaison Officer, National Hi-Tech Crime Unit (NHTCU)

Part 2: Points of exposure

2.1   Email   53
      Indicii Salus
2.2   Web security   61
      Sam Green, Zeus Technology

2.3   Network vulnerabilities   66
        Peter Crowcombe, EMEA Marketing Manager, NetScreen Technologies Inc.
2.4   Remote working   71
        Paul Drew, Tekdata
2.5   Protecting online privacy   73
        Simon Stokes, Tarlo Lyons Solicitors
2.6   Online payments   79
        Colin Whittaker, Head of Security, APACS

        Case Study: Wellbeing.com takes a dose of ClearCommerce medicine   82

        Corporate profile: Proseq   84

Part 3: Software protection

3.1   Intrusion detection   93
        Stuart Eaton, Centrinet
3.2   Firewalls   96
        Stuart Eaton, Centrinet
3.3   Virus attack   98
        Natasha Staley, Anti-Virus Consultant, Sophos Anti-Virus
3.4   Authentication and encryption   102
        Tim Pickard, EMEA Strategic Marketing Director, RSA Security
3.5   Digital signatures   108
        Bart Vansevenant, GlobalSign
3.6   Digital rights   113
        Simon Mehlman, Macrovision
3.7   Electronic licensing   118
        Simon Mehlman, Macrovision

Part 4: Security policies

4.1   Countering cybercrime   125
        The Fraud Advisory Panel, Cybercrime Working Group, ICAEW
4.2   Security as standard   134
        British Standards Institute (BSI)
4.3   Adequate security   139
        Chris Knowles, Computacenter
4.4   A multi-layered response   145
        Paul Barker, Technical Architect, Integralis
4.5   Managed security services   152
        Stuart Eaton, Centrinet
4.6   Security testing   157
        Roy Hills, NTA Monitor
4.7   Open source in the enterprise   160
        Paul Smeddle, Positive Internet Company

Part 5: Organisational back-up

5.1   Employee confidentiality and a culture of security   165
        Peter Wilson, Tarlo Lyons Solicitors
5.2   Electronic contracting   168
        William Kennair (John Venn & Sons, UK), Chair, ICC Commission on
        E-Business, IT and Telecoms Task Force on Security and Authentication
5.3   Information security training   175
        John Harrison, Associate, SAINT and Smart421
5.4   Beyond 'off the shelf'   183
        Ken Watt, INSL

Part 6: Contingency planning

6.1   Business continuity and crisis management   189
        Dr David Smith FBCI, Chair, Education Committee,
        British Continuity Institute
6.2   Data recovery   199
        Gordon Stevenson, Managing Director, Vogon International
6.3   Crisis management   202
        Peter Power, Managing Director, Visor Consultants
6.4   Forensics   207
        Clifford May, Principal Consultant, Integralis

The Power of 2 for
Absolute Peace of Mind

Nokia security appliances enable personal, trusted connections over the Internet for companies of all sizes.

From small offices to carrier-class implementations, our relationship with Check Point Software Technologies helps us to integrate all the capabilities of their software while simplifying deployment.

For more information contact our website **www.nokia.com/internet/emea** or call us at **+44 (0) 161 691 8908.**

Welcome to the real world.

pro|seq

*So **secure** you can **relax***

Internet **insecurity**.

Just one rogue packet – that's all it takes.

– Will you be watching your network when it hits?

Proseq services ensurex 24 x 7 x 365 vigilance and handling!

314
304
294
284
274
264
254
244
234
224
214
204
194
184
174
164
154
144
134
124
114

450 460 470 480 490 500 510 520 530 540 550 560

Foreword

This book explains how technical and operational risks in information security are escalating sharply, with potentially serious strategic consequences.

Hackers, viruses, fraud and denial of service are becoming genuine problems for organisations of all sizes: at a time when companies are expected to have information continuously available for customers, suppliers and partners. In a 24/7 world, the penalties for any downtime are severe: not only causing commercial loss but creating a crisis of confidence in the reliability and security of an organisation. Sadly, this is widely recognised by those who wish to attack an organisation's operation, either with criminal intent or for sheer malevolent satisfaction.

It is often not until an attack has happened or a system has crashed that the full implications for the business become clear. This book is designed to give directors a proper appreciation of the potential risks, explaining where their companies may be vulnerable. Drawing on the expertise of specialists in the area, as well as lawyers, bankers, insurers and business consultants, it examines ways of developing an appropriate security policy.

As the book explains, there is no single cure-all. Effective information security depends on taking a multi-layered approach, combining technical, organisational and legal counter-measures.

Nor, unfortunately, can directors rest there. A continuous process of checking and testing of security needs to be instituted. Slight changes in the configuration of a system can unwittingly create holes through which attacks on data and networks can be launched.

If the worst does happen and there is a major breach of security, then the book reviews the back-up measures that could be put in place and discusses how a crisis can be managed to minimise its impact on the business.

It's unfortunate and frustrating that all the advantages of modern technology have to be accompanied by such consideration. But they have to be faced and dealt with fully.

George Cox
Director General
Institute of Directors

Introduction

The Web is an exciting but unstable place to do business. Both the rewards and risks are high. Security should not be an afterthought in developing a strategy. It is an integral part of setting up sustainable new channels of communication and business. Ignore it at your peril.

Risks to the integrity, availability and confidentiality of e-business activities come in several forms. Some are old threats writ large, such as fraud, espionage and false identities. Others are completely new, like hackers, viruses, spamming and denial of service. None should be underestimated, either alone or in combination. The potential for damage or irretrievable loss is real.

This book is designed as a practical guide for managers in developing and implementing an appropriate response. We first analyse the profile of risks to your business and assess particular areas of exposure, such as email, websites, wireless applications and payment mechanisms. We then review different forms of software protection, including encryption, anti-virus packages and digital signatures. None of these work in isolation, but have to be brought together to form a coherent strategy backed up with appropriate HR and legal policies. Finally, we discuss how to prevent a crisis turning into a disaster and how to retrieve any loss of data.

These contributions draw on a wide range of expertise and know-how both in IT and in other disciplines such as the law, insurance, accounting and consulting. Online security is not just a technical issue, but demands a cross-functional strategic response. The IoD and Kogan Page are grateful to all our contributors for sharing their knowledge so freely and frankly.

Adam Jolly

POLICE

KEEP THE TRAFFIC MOVING ON YOUR NETWORK

The client: Northamptonshire Police Authority – serves over 600,000 people living in the county.

Needed to upgrade IT infrastructure as legacy network was increasingly prone to failure.

Computacenter was selected to fully project manage and install a secure, robust business-critical communications network.

Deployed new standardised desktop and cabling infrastructure across 25 locations to improve performance and lower costs.

Intranet and email facilities enhance information sharing across multiple locations helping the Force to provide a highly responsive service.

Make sure your network's working for your best interests.

IT infrastructure services that consistently deliver

www.computacenter.com/realsolutions
www.northants.police.uk
email: enquiries@computacenter.com

Computacenter

Where vision meets know-how

Information at risk

Secret se▚▚▚▚.

Professional Services, Training, Risk Assessment, Vulnerability and
Penetration Testing, System Security Services, Gap Analysis, BS 7799,
Risk Management, Managed Services and a European Help Desk…
we deliver world-class support services round-the-clock, 365 days a year
(366 in a leap year!). Integralis – *the best kept secret.*

1.1

The business case for information security

In an increasingly connected world where most organisations have some connection to the Internet and many conduct business with their key stake-holders electronically, we have to ask: is our business information at risk? What is the real threat facing UK business? Nick Coleman, Chairman of SAINT (Security Alliance for Internet and New Technologies) and Head of Security Services at IBM, discusses the threat to UK business and how a business case can be built to justify spending on information security.

Is our information at risk?

In the US 90 per cent of organisations surveyed detected computer security breaches during the last 12 months, and a staggering 456 million dollars was reported as having been lost by those organisations as a result (see Figure 1.1.1).

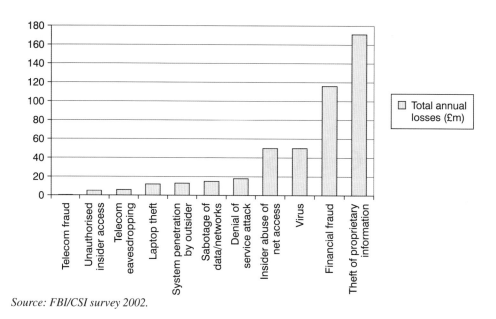

Source: FBI/CSI survey 2002.

Figure 1.1.1 Computer crime costs

These figures also reveal that losses from computer security incidents are at an all time high, as can be seen in Figure 1.1.2.

The most significant area continues to be intellectual property theft, where total losses reported amounted to US$171 million, and the average loss per organisation experiencing these kind of incidents is now some US$6.5 million.

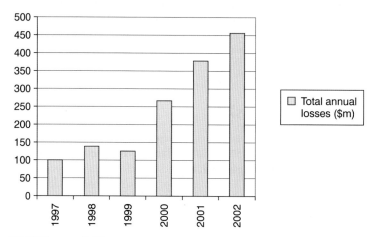

Source: FBI/CSI survey 2002.

Figure 1.1.2 Trends in computer crime costs

With the knowledge that only 503 organisations were surveyed, and only 44 per cent of those organisations were able to quantify their losses, this suggests that total losses for US organisations could run into billions of dollars.

The UK perspective

In 2002, the National Hi-Tech Crime Unit (NHTCU) commissioned NOP to undertake a survey of computer crime in UK organisations. This survey, which I helped the NHTCU commission, was based on the FBI/CSI categories of computer crime, and allowed some new comparisons to be made between the US and UK in this area.

In the last 12 months alone, over 3,000 incidents of computer-enabled crime were experienced by those UK-based organisations surveyed. The NHTCU survey showed that:

■ 67 per cent of organisations surveyed had experienced viruses;
■ 77 per cent had experienced laptop thefts;
■ 20 per cent had experienced a denial of service attack.

Denial of service attacks are those where the perpetrator repeatedly sends vast amounts of data packets to flood a system or complete network with the intention of degrading performance or shutting it down.

Virus attacks were still the most frequently occurring incidents, with 1612 incidents taking place during the last 12 months alone.[1]

In the FBI/CSI 2002 survey:

■ 85 per cent of organisations surveyed had experienced viruses;
■ 55 per cent had experienced laptop thefts;
■ 40 per cent has experienced a denial of service attack.

Before making direct comparisons we need to take into account the differences in sample populations. For example, there were 105 organisations surveyed in this initial NHTCU/NOP survey and 503 organisations surveyed in the FBI/CSI 2002 survey. However, we can see that in the United States 18 per cent more organisations reported experiencing viruses, double the number of US organisations experienced a denial of service attack, and 22 per cent fewer organisations reported suffering laptop thefts.

The cost to UK business

The NHTCU survey did not attempt to calculate the losses to UK organisations from these kinds of crime. However, the survey did provide us with some base data upon which certain assumptions can be applied, making it possible to place a figure on how much we might assume was lost by UK businesses from computer-enabled crime incidents during the last 12 months.

---

[1] NHTCU/NOP survey 2002.

If we assume that the average loss to businesses in the UK would have been at the same levels as those losses experienced by US organisations, we can estimate the losses to UK business.

Sizing the impact from virus incidents

Using this approach, if 67 per cent of the organisations reported experiencing virus attacks in the UK during the last 12 months,[2] this would equate to 70 companies. Multiplying this number by the average loss per organisation allows us to derive the total potential loss from viruses for those organisations surveyed.

The FBI/CSI survey identified that 428 organisations surveyed experienced a virus incident, but only 188 organisations were able to quantify the costs of such incidents. Among those 188 organisations, the highest loss experienced was US$9 million and the average loss was some US$283,000. Multiplying US$283,000 by 70 gives a total loss for the surveyed organisations based in the UK of some 20 million dollars.

Calculating the total cost to UK business

Using the same method for each of the categories of computer crime, we can calculate the losses that might be expected across all categories for the 105 organisations surveyed (see Figure 1.1.3).

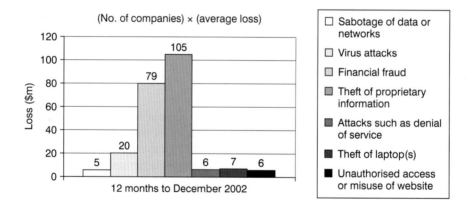

Sources: NHTCU/NOP survey 2002; FBI/CSI survey 2002.

Figure 1.1.3 Cost of computer crime (UK)

Totalled together this would equate to US$228 million being lost by the UK businesses surveyed over the last 12 months. However, this figure does need to be treated with great caution, and should not be taken to be statistically significant.

---

[2] NHTCU/NOP survey 2002.

The NHTCU/NOP survey only dealt with 105 organisations and was never meant to draw statistical conclusions, and getting to this figure is only achieved when a number of assumptions are made. Furthermore, this calculation may be too conservative.

■ There were 129 instances of theft of hardware other than laptops. These incidents are omitted from the US$228 million methodology, as we had no information on the average losses for this kind of incident.
■ 63 per cent of organisations surveyed in the FBI/CSI survey of 2002 had 1000 or more employees whereas 82 per cent of those surveyed in the NHTCU/NOP survey had 1000 or more employees.
■ Larger organisations are expected to have higher losses, and therefore the average loss should be higher for the UK sample having more large organisations, and, if true, this would inflate the US$228 million total loss calculated for UK organisations.

Even if this number is not accurate, what we can deduce is that with over 3000 incidents and losses estimated here of some US$228 million for 105 organisations, there is a significant threat from this type of crime in the UK, and organisations need to be prepared for such incidents. But at what level do they need to plan, and how can we calculate the specific threat to one organisation?

Making this specific to one organisation

To calculate this, an organisation needs to conduct a formal risk assessment. In doing a risk assessment it is possible to determine, amongst other things, the potential impact of an incident for the organisation, and the probability of that impact occurring. These two figures, when multiplied together, provide one view on the level of threat that exists for those incidents.

Probability times impact

The threat level described above (probability the impact will occur times impact) will need to be calculated with data relevant to the organisation's own environment. Before we look at how this specific data might be calculated, we should look at how a probability times impact model might work.

An industry generic example

If 20 per cent of UK organisations suffered a denial of service attack in the last 12 months, then the probability of an organisation being attacked is 20 per cent. Assuming that the average company loss for this type of incident is US$300,000 as reported in the FBI/CSI survey 2002, by multiplying the probability of 20 per cent by the average loss US$300,000 for this type of incident we can see that the perceived threat level would be around US$60,000.

Reading this, it is clear to a large organisation that a successful denial of service attack would cost the company much more, and this re-enforces the need for information specific to the company in question, something which will be covered in the next section.

Figure 1.1.4 shows the results using the same approach for denial of service attacks with all categories of computer crime.

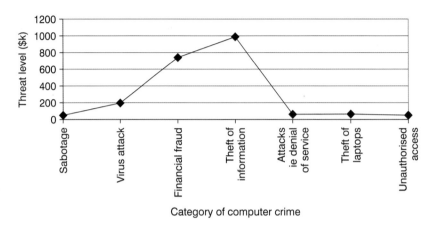

Figure 1.1.4 Cost of computer crime (impact times probability)

Tailoring this model to your own organisation environment

Using data specific to your own organisation is essential. For example, does the average loss from the industry reflect the impact that might be felt in your organisation? And how can you calculate the probability without factoring in the specifics of your own organisation and the environment it is operating in?

Calculating the probability of an impact occurring in your organisation

To get to this organisation-specific data, let us consider the probability perspective first. What is the probability that incidents will occur in any particular organisation? With over 3,000 incidents occurring in the UK and only three per cent of organisations not having experienced any incidents of computer crime in the last 12 months, you have to start by assuming it might happen to you.

At the same time, it is not practical to assume that every incident will affect every organisation. You have to be prepared for all kinds of incidents – but an organisation without a website would not be susceptible to a website defacement, etc.

Using a risk assessment process enables the organisation to understand a more realistic probability of an impact occurring. My methodology for doing this takes into account many factors including technologies used, geographical location, security policy etc to calculate a realistic probability that the impact might occur.

Sizing the potential impact on your organisation

Looking next at the impact of an incident, how can we determine the potential impact of a denial of service incident or a virus attack on an organisation? It must be said upfront that it is often not possible to completely size the impact that may be experienced in the organisation from, say, a virus attack. However, from our understanding of the cost of down-time in an organisation, we have a base set of categories to work from in order to calculate the impact of an incident (see Figure 1.1.5).

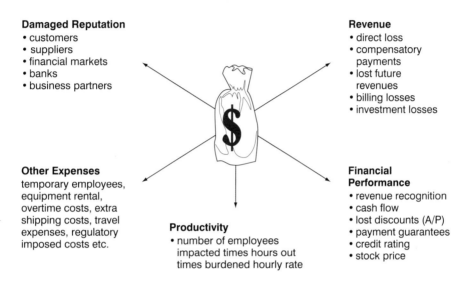

Figure 1.1.5 Cost of down-time

These factors allow us to see where the impact might come from. To calculate the impact, we need to understand what assets might be affected by an incident, then calculate the impact that an incident might have upon those assets. There are several types of asset that need to be considered in doing this. Section 5 of the BS 7799: Part 1 Code of Practice for Information Security Management is a good reference on this area if you are looking for an independent source of data.

Finally, when it comes to actually sizing the impact, companies often say it is difficult to get data from within their organisation, and if you find the same in your organisation then the average loss figure that the FBI/CSI survey refers to, may be a good starting point. Then over time you can capture information that would validate this figure within your own organisation, determining which assets are likely to be affected and what impact – looking at the categories in Figure 1.1.5 – might be experienced.

Other aspects to consider

In the above methodology we have only factored in the negative impact of security breaches; we have not taken into account the fact that making security investments can have positive impacts on the brand, reduce operating costs of a business etc. In building the return on investment (ROI) for an organisation, positive and negative benefits need to be taken into account. The method works in much the same way, multiplying the size of the positive impact by the probability that that positive impact will be experienced.

Forming the ROI case

The above method has introduced one way of capturing some numerical information about the level of threat to your organisation. The next step is to decide if that is an acceptable level of risk for the organisation. The organisation needs to make a decision as to whether it wants to accept that risk, or put solutions in place to mitigate that risk. Security programmes, if properly executed, will enable the organisation to reduce the impact and/or the probability of an incident occurring, and it is against this context that an organisation can produce a return of investment case. However, there is always a certain level of residual risk that the organisation has to accept, even after having made its security investments. There is no such thing as 100 per cent security.

Other ways to calculate the ROI to the organisation

There are a number of different approaches that could have been demonstrated here but the purpose of this chapter was to share the new information that has been provided by the NHTCU/NOP survey and to show how it can assist us in building the business case for security.

In the work group at SAINT (Security Alliance for Internet and New Technologies) we are considering all these different approaches, and we will publish a White Paper on this subject during 2003 which will cover the different approaches in more detail, including one that is based on BS 7799.

Final thoughts

The NHTCU/NOP survey revealed 34 per cent of organisations are spending under one per cent of their total spend on computer security, 46 per cent are spending under two per cent and 22 per cent of respondents were spending between two and five per cent. Given that there were over 3,000 incidents reported by those same 105 organisations in the last 12 months, organisations should perhaps be regularly reviewing their spending levels. Performing regular risk assessments of the kind that I have described here can help you get this process started in your organisation.

Nick Coleman is Chairman of SAINT (Security Alliance for Internet and New Technologies) and Head of Security Services at IBM. He is a panel member on the CBI committee on Information Security, Trust and Risk Management, and a member of the Advisory Board of the Computer Security Research Centre at the London School of Economics. If you would like more detail on Nick's approach to calculating the cost of computer crime please email him on coleman@uk.ibm.com.

SAINT was launched in December 2001 by the then Minister for E-commerce, Douglas Alexander MP, to raise awareness and promote best practice in information security. It is uniquely positioned among security organisations, having representatives from across business, government and vendors amongst its membership. Its governing committee demonstrates this with representatives from the Cabinet Office, DTI, CBI, IBM, Symantec, Smart421and Microsoft. For further information on SAINT visit www.uksaint.org.

The demand for continuous information

Recent world events have demonstrated the serious disruption that can be caused by a break in information flow in a 24-hour, seven-days-a-week global economy, writes Rick Cudworth, Partner at KPMG.

If there's one thing that's certain when it comes to developments in business technology, it's that 24/7 system availability will continue to be at the top of the business agenda. Now more than ever, interaction between customer and company takes place through technological channels, be they call-centres, email or the Internet. These channels have overtaken traditional face-to-face contact.

Over the next five years the importance of these channels to customer communication and quality of service will increase, simply because they allow businesses to become more accessible to their customers in a highly cost-efficient way. But, despite this, few companies are able to measure the cost of IT failure to the business, and with the range of security threats that can bring a business down, information availability remains a tough nut to crack.

Recent world events, regulatory pressures and stronger corporate governance mean that business continuity has again become a hot topic. The difference is that now the risks and threats are greater and unspecific, organisations are even more dependent on complex technology and, with the growth of the Internet to support customer transactions and relationships, they are increasingly intolerant of down-time.

The growing challenge of 24/7 availability

In the summer of 2002, KPMG conducted a survey of FTSE senior executives on the importance of different customer contact channels to their businesses. The key findings reinforce the growing supremacy of technology in facilitating this interaction, and the ongoing difficulties faced by businesses in measuring costs.

■ Of those surveyed, 94 per cent of businesses said that their customers now use call centres to contact them, with 88 per cent of those questioned using email and 66 per cent also using the Internet. This compares with more traditional methods, where only 43 per cent of customers still use branch networks. What's more, 38 per cent of companies now also generate up to 10 per cent of their revenue via the Internet.

■ When questioned on the need for 24/7 access, 52 per cent of respondents described continuous information availability as critical to customer service today, rising to 85 per cent when asked if it would be critical in three years time. This underscores the premise that continuous customer access to information will be a growing requirement, and that continuous system and information availability across multiple channels will be imperative.

■ However, despite the growing importance of 'always open' technology channels, 75 per cent of businesses had no way of measuring the cost of IT failure to the business, although 80 per cent felt that it would be beneficial to be able to better relate the performance of IT to quality of service.

■ Equally, while 69 per cent did have technology-based service level agreements in place to help monitor IT performance, only 23 per cent actually employed metrics to measure the cost of IT failure. Half of these had lost more than £100,000 from IT failures in the last year, owing to loss of sales and customers or due to service penalties incurred.

The research shows that whilst organisations are striving to improve information availability to customers, and do recognise that technology failures will directly and materially impact on service to customers, they still need to take more vigorous steps to monitor IT performance and be able to directly link it to business performance. What's more, as the range and severity of security threats grow, the need to have effective means of protecting the IT infrastructure and, therefore, continuous availability becomes imperative.

11/09/01 – The world has changed

Nobody could have predicted the disaster that hit the World Trade Center in September 2001. It was an unprecedented event and even the most thorough business continuity efforts could not have prepared for such a widespread disaster scenario. However, a number of lessons learned from this event are significantly changing the way we look at business continuity and system availability.

The first major differential was the scale of the disaster. The entire Manhattan business district was evacuated, leading hundreds of firms to invoke their recovery arrangements and attempt to relocate to alternative sites. Many firms had contracts for syndicated space at recovery sites outside Manhattan, but found that they had been beaten to it by other firms when they attempted to invoke because the recovery companies had sold the same space numerous times to firms within the same area. Despite their hefty annual payments, organisations had no guarantee of recovery space.

Secondly, until this point there had been a general move towards consolidation of space and centralisation of group functions. What was seen during the World Trade Center disaster was that those firms that had distributed functions (for example, where two mirrored data centres based in different locations shared the day-to-day load of the business) could continue to operate seamlessly, even if one location suffered a total outage for a number of days. Firms are now readdressing their longer-term strategies and are building continuity back into their day-to-day business operations.

Lessons for availability

There is a variety of business continuity strategies that organisations can adopt. At a high level, these range from resiliency-based rapid recovery options through to plan-based slower recovery options. These options come at great variances in cost, and one of the greatest challenges lies in deciding how much to invest in business continuity.

Some different recovery strategies include:

■ a mirrored site for immediate failover with minimal downtime;
■ an outsourced hot site – a dedicated space with the technological infrastructure set up and ready for restoration of the last day's data;
■ an owned site in a different risk zone (ie not in an area likely to be affected by the same risks) for use as a back-up;
■ a reciprocal agreement with another organisation to provide recovery workspace;
■ a cold site where equipment and communications will be sourced and installed when needed at the time of the incident.

The level of recovery that is most appropriate to your organisation depends on how much down-time you can tolerate and the complexity of the technology and operations that support your critical activities. If you can survive without operating a business activity for up to five days without incurring major loss then you should look to develop sound back-up and recovery plans and procedures that are thoroughly tested and proven, and good contingency plans for business recovery.

If you cannot tolerate down-time in excess of a few hours, and you depend on complex technology, a strategy that includes a degree of technological and operational resilience will be essential, since traditional recovery will not satisfy your requirements. This is likely to include investment in an IT infrastructure that will replicate and maintain the availability of your information in close to real-time.

It is important to remember that in most cases one approach will not be appropriate for every business area. For example, your treasury function may require a high resilience solution involving substantial investment, whereas your back-office functions may be recovered successfully within a week through the use of recovery plans and procedures. However, it should be noted that with ever-more integrated systems it is becoming difficult to apply different recovery and back-up strategies to individual applications, and a strategy for the supporting infrastructure as a whole is increasingly necessary. A business impact assessment is key to helping an organisation invest wisely in business continuity and technology recovery, neither over- nor under-investing.

Steps for protection

So what steps can you take to protect against down-time and ensure maximum availability? There is no single solution to business continuity that can be applied to all organisations. Each company should develop its own arrangements that are appropriate to the size and nature of its operations, its risk profile and its appetite for risk against cost of building and maintaining business continuity.

The approach laid out in Figure 1.2.1 is organised into four phases that are executed in sequence and thereafter on a cyclical basis. Each phase is broken down into activities and tasks with practical issues and guidance alongside. The steps may be amended to suit, and may be pre-determined by individual methods and tools already in place.

Challenging your business continuity and information availability arrangements

Business continuity arrangements must be continually assessed, refined and improved. As you assess your contingency plans going forward, it can help to keep in mind the following critical questions, which will help you to strive for continual improvement of your business continuity capabilities:

■ Is your business continuity strategy event-driven or risk-driven and stakeholder focused?
■ How critical is information availability to your success?
■ Are capabilities for managing business continuity aligned with organisational strategy?
■ Who are your stakeholders and what is their tolerance for unplanned downtime?
■ Does your risk management programme address people, processes and technology as well as the extended enterprise?
■ Does your business continuity strategy eliminate single points of failure?
■ How do you reinforce key management disciplines to ensure reliable service delivery to all stakeholders?
■ Are you maximising the use of your facilities to provide the best possible business continuity structure?
■ How do you optimise the value of information flowing across the value chain?
■ Does management have timely and independent assurance that its business continuity capabilities are adequate?

Conclusion

Over the next five years the criticality of technology channels to providing multiple customer touch-points and, therefore, better service will continue to increase. Down-time is not an option, and this has significant implications for IT-related business continuity, security and risk management. It is no small undertaking, but by following the right steps it should not be too costly or too difficult a problem to solve.

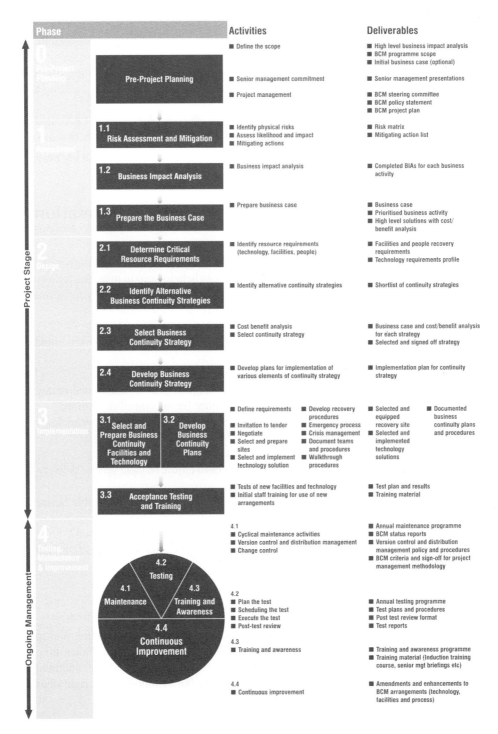

Figure 1.2.1 Four-phase approach to business continuity

Useful links

UK links

www.kpmg.co.uk – the website of KPMG containing details of their products and services and how to contact them for further information.

www.thebci.co.uk – the homepage of the Business Continuity Institute who provide the only recognised accreditation for business continuity practitioners in the UK.

www.survive.com – this website of the membership group for business continuity professionals is a good source of background material, articles, training courses and career information.

www.globalcontinuity.com – this is a global portal for business continuity and IT disaster recovery. You can register here for news and articles relating to all aspects of business continuity and disaster recovery.

www.cityoflondon.gov.uk – the Corporation of London's Security and Contingency Planning Group is available to assist businesses in the City with the development and exercising of their business continuity plans.

www.ukresilience.info/londonprepared – this website was set up by the government after 11 September 2001 to ensure that London is prepared for an emergency.

US links

www.availability.com – a research site on technology availability and business continuity, which also provides tools such as the 'Availability Cost Justifier' and discussions on such areas as the White Paper.

www.disasterrecoveryworld.com – a directory of business continuity and disaster recovery software and services.

www.bcpbenchmark.com – a survey conducted by KPMG and *Contingency Planning and Management* magazine containing useful statistics about many aspects of business continuity management across different industries in the US (eg organisational structure, frequent failures, RTOs, costs of disruption, methods of maintenance etc).

KPMG is the global network of professional services firms whose aim is to turn knowledge into value for the benefit of its clients, its people and its communities. KPMG LLP operates from 24 offices across the UK with more than 9,500 partners and staff. KPMG recorded a UK fee income of £1,373 million in the year ended September 2001. KPMG LLP is a UK limited liability partnership and the UK member of KPMG International, a Swiss non-operating association.

For further information on availability services contact Rick Cudworth on 0117 905 4005.

The threat from cybercrime

Hackers; e-theft; netspionage; domain scams; telecoms; credit cards. The Fraud Advisory Panel of the Cybercrime Working Group at the ICAEW reports on where companies are finding themselves vulnerable.

Hackers

Hackers divide into two main groups. The internal hacker and the external hacker. The hacker may work as an individual or in highly organised gangs, either of whom may attempt to gain access into a computer system in order to carry out a criminal activity. The hacker may intend to steal information or funds, to publicise a cause (more commonly known as 'hactivism') or to deface a website. Some hackers claim to hack the sites of software developers and others in order to prove that security can be violated and to highlight security flaws.

In January 2002 hackers cut off the website of the World Economic Forum through a 'denial of service' attack, disrupting a conference of world political and economic leaders. In the previous year, the hackers broke into the site and stole details of 27,000 delegates attending the conference. The Department of Trade and Industry (DTI) Report[1] of April 2002 reveals that key UK government departments face an average of 84 hacking attempts a week.

---

[1] Information Security Breaches Survey 2002, DTI. Original source: 'Hackers target UK national infrastructure', Andy McCue, vnu.net.com report, 26 March 2002.

Web sabotage is a major cause of concern for the Police. Hackers access genuine websites and alter their appearance, change information or set up a replica website using false information. A recent example of web sabotage involved the Red Cross website. The site was cloned by hackers following the events of September 11th and for 36 hours all donations made to the Red Cross were diverted to a cyber-fraudster.

Internal hackers do not have to penetrate the system from the outside. It is therefore far easier for an internal hacker to cause damage. PricewaterhouseCoopers reported in June 2001 that 60 per cent of frauds were committed internally. It has also been reported that up to 75 per cent of thefts and frauds have been committed by an insider.

E-theft

It was reported[2] in early 2001 that an employee of an oil company managed to steal US$473,541 through e-theft. She transferred funds from the company to her husband's business in two electronic transactions over an 11-month period. The fraud took so long to uncover because of the procedures adopted by the company. The broker handling accounts never received a list of authorised accounts to which he could transfer funds, and because duties in the company were segregated, the left hand didn't know what the right hand was doing!

In January 2002, it was reported by Evans Data[3] that 27 per cent of US and Canadian banks suffered a hack attempt during 2001.

Netspionage

Netspionage is where confidential information is stolen from a company by hackers, to sell to a competitor or for the use of individuals in their business exploits. Espionage was originally limited to governments, but in the information age the rise of corporate espionage has been rapid.

In March 2001 it was reported[4] that an unidentified hacker escaped with the system codes for satellite and missile guidance systems. The theft was not even discovered until three days after it had happened. It was widely suspected that the information was to be used for the purposes of industrial espionage.

According to recent surveys, worldwide losses suffered through misappropriation of computerised intellectual property cost copyright owners close to US$20 billion last year.

Canal Plus is suing NDS Group plc for US$3 billion for allegedly sabotaging its business. It is alleged that NDS obtained the security code on the Canal Plus smartcard, which gave viewers a choice of different channels. Whilst many companies engage in reverse-engineering to examine their competitors' products, Canal Plus claims that NDS

---

[2] *All Wired Up*, 'Electronic funds transfers are prime targets', Joseph R Dervaes, Association of Fraud Examiners, 2001.

[3] *Newsbytes*, '27% of US Canadian Banking Databases Breached', Dick Kelsey, Evans Data Corp, 22 January 2002.

[4] 'Hacker nabs top secret US space codes', ZDNet UK News, 2 March 2001.

published the security code on the Internet, where it was picked up by international counter-feiters. In turn, it is alleged that the counterfeiters produced fake smartcards that allowed users to watch subscription channels free. Canal Plus says that this was a deliberate plan to sabotage the business in which it was a market leader. The allegations have been denied.

In a report[5] by the Confederation of British Industry (CBI) in August 2001, six per cent of UK respondents reported that they had suffered from netspionage, and quantifiable losses were set at £151 million compared to £66 million in the same report in the previous year.

Domain name renewal scams

A recent scam to emerge concerns domain name renewal. This has been a concern in both the US and Europe. A victim will commonly receive an email from a sender who is purportedly a domain name registrar. The registrar offers you an opportunity to upgrade your website address with the new suffix '.info'. The email will include a hyperlink to allow you to read more information about the upgrade; however when you enter the link the program functions as if you had agreed to transfer your domain name. The domain name is then transferred to their company as registrar, who claim that you requested the transfer.

Telecom fraud

Telecom fraud is a less well-known method of committing e-theft. This method is estimated to net organised gangs of fraudsters £40 billion a year. One method used is 'phreaking' which is the equivalent of hacking on computer networks. A company's telephone exchange is penetrated using a computer program which permits the calls to be resold to other users. Usually a cheap telephone company is set up offering international calls at a very low cost. In one case this type of fraud cost a business £750,000 in extra telephone calls.

A different type of telecom fraud is known as 'premium rate' fraud. Businesses are particularly susceptible to this kind of fraud, which involves an employee dialling a premium rate number at night and leaving the telephone off the hook. The employee's accomplice will have set up the premium rate number and then charges the company for the cost of the telephone call.

Identity/credit card fraud

Online retail has made the life of the credit card fraudster far easier due to the degree of anonymity permitted. There are a number of methods of obtaining credit card details, from the low-tech methods of 'bin-raiding' to the high-tech methods of 'cloning', 'skimming' and obtaining details by hacking into websites.

The fraudster then carries out online purchases using the credit card details and requesting that the goods are sent to a different address to that of the genuine card holder.

---

[5] *The Cybercrime Survey 2001*, CBI.

The credit card holder eventually discovers that a number of purchases have been made on their card fraudulently. The credit card company generally reimburses the credit card holder's account, but the retailer usually foots the bill due to the terms and conditions of the contract they have with credit card companies. This is commonly known as a 'charge back'.

In March 2002, the Association for Payment Clearing Services (APACS) reported that credit card fraud in the UK had cost £400 million. Card-not-present fraud, which is carried out over the telephone or the Internet, rose by 94 per cent in 2000 and is one of the fastest growing types of fraud in the UK. Credit card fraud has been estimated to reach £600 million per year in the UK by 2005.

The Institute of Chartered Accountants in England and Wales (ICAEW) is the largest professional accountancy body in Europe, with over 122,000 members. For more information on its Fraud Advisory Panel email info@fraudadvisorypanel.org

Recent attack trends

Attack tools are becoming easier to source, quicker to deploy and are evolving at a rate that allows them to bypass traditional security measures, writes Stuart Eaton from Centrinet.

Trends

Whilst the Internet has created a number of opportunities for companies to save costs and improve marketing, at the same time it has exposed companies to much greater risk to both their cost-base and brand. Below are some of the more common ways in which companies can suffer from the more disreputable section of the 'information society'.

Trend 1: Automation and speed of attack tools

The level of automation in attack tools continues to increase. Automated attacks commonly involve four phases, each of which is changing:

- scanning for potential victims;
- compromising vulnerable systems;
- propagation of the attack;
- co-ordinated management of attack tools.

Trend 2: Increasing sophistication of attack tools

Attack tool developers are using more advanced techniques than previously, including:

- anti-forensics;
- dynamic behaviour;
- modularity of attack tools.

Trend 3: Faster discovery of vulnerabilities

The number of newly discovered vulnerabilities reported to the CERT/CC (CERT Co-ordination Centre) continues to more than double each year.[1] It is difficult for administrators to keep up to date with patches. Additionally, new classes of vulnerabilities are discovered each year.

Trend 4: Increasing permeability of firewalls

Firewalls are often relied upon to provide primary protection from intruders. However, technologies such as IPP (Internet Printing Protocol) and WebDAV (Web-based Distributed Authoring and Versioning), as well as certain protocols marketed as being firewall-friendly, are designed to bypass typical firewall configurations.

Trend 5: Increasingly asymmetric threat

Security on the Internet is, by its very nature, highly interdependent. Because of the advances in attack technology, a single attacker can easily employ a large number of distributed systems to launch devastating attacks against a single victim.

Trend 6: Increasing threat from infrastructure attacks

Infrastructure attacks broadly affect key components of the Internet. Three types of infrastructure attack are:

■ distributed denial of service;
■ worms;
■ attacks on the Internet Domain Name System (DNS).

Proliferation of attack tools and 'script kiddies'

'Script kiddies' can be thought of as cyber joyriders. They are often not looking for a specific company or seeking particular information. They focus on using a small number of known vulnerabilities and scan indiscriminately in order to find and exploit them.

A small minority of script kiddies possess the required technical knowledge to produce the scripts they use. The majority, however, will use ready-made tools that are easily downloadable from the Internet. Perversely this majority can be the most dangerous as they lack the required understanding of the effect of their actions on corporate systems. Regardless of which camp the script kiddies fall into, they often default to the same strategy, namely a random search for a specific weakness followed by exploitation.

The fact that the attacks and scans are random means that the script kiddies are a threat. As night follows day, your systems will be scanned. Projects, such as Honeynet, have taken place that concluded that an average system is often scanned seven to eight times a day. This pattern further underlines the proliferation of automated tools that scan whole IP (Internet Protocol) ranges for vulnerabilities.

---

[1] 'Overview of attack trends', CERT.

PoizonB0x, a notorious group of hackers, created iisautoexp.pl, an automated tool that handles all the groundwork required to gain access to sites and perform defacing operations. To deface a website the user simply has to give the name of the website to the script and then run it. If the website is vulnerable the front page is changed to read 'PoizonB0x Ownz YA' (sic). A known tactic is to create files with the names of target websites, thereby producing mass defacement.

The frightening fact is that, with so many users on the Internet employing these tools, it is no longer a question of if you will be probed, but when; and if the vulnerabilities are there they will be found and exploited. Indeed the Computer Security Institute (CSI) reported[2] that 85 per cent of primarily large corporations and government agencies detected computer security breaches within the last 12 months.

Lack of awareness of the value of data

The realisation of the value of data has been slow in coming. The retail industry realised that by introducing loyalty cards they could gain intelligence on customers and then use it to better target marketing and improve their understanding of buying relationships and trends. This data was worth millions and, it is claimed, allowed Tesco to overtake Sainsbury's in the UK supermarket sector.

In what Microsoft has called a 'deplorable act of industrial espionage', their network was compromised and it is suspected that attackers may have stolen source codes to some of Microsoft's products. The attack was first noticed when passwords were seen leaving the Microsoft campus, destined for a location in St Petersburg, Russia.[3]

A 2001 FBI and CSI report[4] listed the most serious financial losses that occurred through theft of proprietary information (34 respondents reported US$151,230,100) and financial fraud (21 respondents reported US$92,935,500).

Companies increasingly trade on brand

How much is a brand name worth? Corporate accountants claim that they are worth billions, and corporate lawyers spend millions on defending them. *Business Week*[5] believes that the top two global brands, Coca-Cola and Microsoft, are worth over US$60 billion each.

The protection of brand names therefore is of critical concern. During the Firestone scandal, analysts predicted that the Ford motor company brand would lose up to US$6.3 billion in market value.

Whilst the Internet has given companies a cost-effective and powerful platform on which to market and to establish brand value, it has in turn exposed brands to greater risk. The very fact that hacking tools are freely available and are in essence automatic makes

---

[2] '2001Computer Crime and Security Survey', CSI/FBI.
[3] Reuters, 27 October 2000.
[4] '2001Computer Crime and Security Survey', CSI/FBI.
[5] *Business Week*, 'The world's 10 most valuable brands', Interbrand Corp., JP Morgan Chase & Co.

them ideal for groups with a specific grudge against a company. The anti-capitalism movement has long been aware of the power of hacking. At the World Economic Forum in Switzerland in 2001, a man was arrested due to his part in a hack that allowed access to dignitaries' credit card details, which were then delivered to a newspaper. The political motivations of this were mentioned during the case.

The following cases further illustrate the risk:

■ A hacker/extortionist breached security at the online electronics store TheNerds.net, making off with customer credit card information. The thief sent emails to some of the affected customers. TheNerds.net is notifying all its customers that their personal data may have been compromised. The hacker allegedly broke into the site through an SQL (structured query language) server. The company will not meet any extortion demand and is working with the FBI and the US Secret Service on the case. Someone using the same hacker handle broke into three other websites over the past eight months, and has demanded up to US$50,000 to keep quiet about the breach.

■ On 21 June 2000, the domain name 'nike.com' was hijacked and redirected to a new site dedicated to a protest that occurred on 11 September 2000. Nike successfully regained control of their domain by 12pm that day, but visitors were still receiving the hijacked information for some time afterwards.

■ During the second week of February 2001, hackers broke into such prominent websites as the *New York Times*, Compaq, Intel, AltaVista, Hewlett-Packard and Go.Com.

Centrinet are a leading provider of Internet and network security solutions based on the innovative use of the best products and services. Our passion for customer service and technical excellence, combined with a no-nonsense approach to business, provides our clients with a refreshing and unique experience.

For further information contact: Centrinet Limited, Witham Park House, Waterside South, Lincoln, Lincolnshire LN5 7JN. Tel: +44 (0)1522 559 600; Fax: +44 (0)1522 533 745; Email: enquiries@centri.net; Website: www.centri.net

Recognising the enemy within

To do their jobs efficiently people are placed in a position of trust, with access to sensitive data and systems. You cannot just rely on their goodwill, says Declan Grogan at Security Designers. Temporary, careless or rogue employees can cause real problems.

The scale of the internal problem

Too often companies prefer to look outward when it comes to problems such as hacking when, in reality, problems could be based closer to home.

Last year hackers cost business US$45 billion – according to PricewaterhouseCoopers. Research by the FBI as far back as its 1997 survey was also extremely worrying.

The Computer Security Institute (CSI) in San Francisco teamed with the Computer Crime Squad of the FBI in 1997 to undertake the second FBI/CSI Computer Crime Survey. The sampling base included 5,000 information security professionals, of which 563 completed the survey. From these organisations, 249 reported losses of over US$100 million from computer crime.

Average losses by category included:

- financial fraud: 26 responses averaging US$957,384;
- theft of proprietary information: 21 responses averaging US$954,666;
- telecommunications fraud: 35 responses averaging US$647,437;

- unauthorised access: 22 responses averaging US$181,436;
- sabotage: 14 responses averaging US$164,840;
- system penetration: 22 responses averaging US$132,250.

The survey also reported that 64 per cent of respondents said they experienced computer security breaches within the last 12 months. The problem of employees – 'insiders' – was underscored in several parts of the survey. For example, 44 per cent reported unauthorised access by employees, and the most serious financial losses occurred through unauthorised access by insiders (18 respondents reported a total of US$50,565,000 in losses), theft of proprietary information (20 respondents reported a total of US$33,545,000 in losses), telecommunications fraud (32 respondents reported a total of US$17,256,000 in losses) and financial fraud (29 respondents reported a total of US$11,239,000 in losses).

Conspiracy or complacency?

It should be recognised that to allow people to do their jobs efficiently we have to place them in a position of trust, with access to sensitive data and systems. Given the evidence, however, it is no longer adequate to rely purely on goodwill and faith. There are a number of areas that provide potential risks.

Temporary staff

At times of peak load, temporary staff often arrive on site on the first day, direct from the supply agency, without interview or other screening process. Of course they come with the Microsoft Word and Excel skills that we specifically asked for, and that is demonstrable in minutes, but what other skills are they also armed with? Having probably worked in a greater variety of environments they are probably more adept at finding their way into non-protected space. What privileges do we ask our network administrators to give these people when, after all, we expect them to do the same work as a full-time member of staff?

Rogue and careless employees

The obvious primary candidate in this category is the disgruntled employee, overlooked for promotion, supposedly undervalued, denied a reserved car parking space, or just plain got out of bed on the wrong side. The next candidates in this category are under-utilised employees who find themselves with time on their hands during the working day in which to experiment and investigate. For whatever reason, at a given moment in time they are not the best friends of the company.

The careless employee is the one that leaves their password written on a piece of paper in the top drawer of their desk, or who walks away from a terminal leaving it connected to a valuable data source. The careless employee is not necessarily malicious and in most cases is not aware of the potential impact of their actions, because nobody has made it clear to them.

Whatever the nature of the internal breach, the cost of remedying the damage done is potentially very high – assuming that you are even aware that the breach has occurred.

Passwords

This may seem simple, but passwords must be employed, as well as systems armed with screen savers that require passwords to unlock them. It is no use having implemented this technology if you then write the password on the whiteboard by the desk or tell all your friends what it is. There are technologies that can help in this area, such as biometrics, proximity badges or token-based systems, but staff education is the most effective solution.

Viruses

Apart from the well-known damage that viruses can cause, what is less-known is that some viruses sit passively and send sensitive information back out to sites and hackers on the Internet, or open up doorways for incoming connections. This information is often used for more serious security breaches and, as you are generating the information internally and sending it out, your firewall systems often pass it on unaware of its true nature. It was just such a virus (or 'Trojans' as they are known) that allegedly struck inside Microsoft last year, potentially exposing some of their source code – the company's 'crown jewels' as it were – to parties unknown.

SpyWare

To continue on this theme, there are many software applications that also broadcast information out in a similar way. Often based in games or 'utilities' that are downloaded from the Internet or brought into the office, they act in exactly the same way as many of the Trojan viruses.

Internet surfing

Is it fraud to spend your employer's time surfing the Internet for private use? Of people with access to the Internet 54 per cent spend at least 30 minutes a day 'surfing' for private purposes. The same survey shows that 70 per cent of pornography downloaded over the Internet is downloaded at work. Given the ability to import Trojans and viruses, and the loss of productivity involved, Internet access should be seriously monitored and the rules of its usage clearly understood. Managers also need to be aware that there are sites out there that can glean a lot of information about your network by simply attaching to them or following the downloading of objects into a web browser.

There are many packages available for managing this problem, including regularly updated access control lists. However, they are only part of the armoury and a firm, clearly communicated policy, with the user's knowledge that auditing is available, is used and that the company's 'acceptable usage policy' is enforced, significantly reduces this threat.

Email

We all love to gossip, and email has certainly improved and informalised the way we communicate with each other. With this ease and openness comes a significant threat. How do you stop company confidential information disappearing out onto the Internet at the touch of a button? Or stop the joke application that is sent to you by a friend downloading information via a Trojan to a hacker on the Internet?

Virus protection certainly has to be a priority here, on both the workstations and the mail servers. Careful consideration should also be given as to who should be able to send mail attachments, and also to the implementation of scanners that check mail content to stop people sending out unauthorised confidential material.

Another threat associated with email, and one that has led to well-documented cases of very costly lawsuits, is that of email content and defamatory remarks being issued via corporate email to the outside world. The word 'policy' applies here as elsewhere.

Poor network policy

Modern PC systems are designed to talk to each other very easily, and the average school leaver has plenty of familiarity with them. The ability to browse the internal network opens up the possibility of seeing data on all sorts of internal systems and other users' PCs. It is quite conceivable that in a poorly secured environment a user could gain access to the information held on a senior manager's PC.

The paper copies of the management accounts of a business are kept under lock and key, but often it is easy to access this information on poorly secured servers or PCs. This is worsened by the fact that all sorts of tools can be downloaded along with documented back-doors into desktop and server operating systems. Once again, policy along with appropriate traffic management and auditing go a long way to protecting sensitive data.

Policy does not apply to me!

Having a policy is all well and good, but it must be enforced. Often threats can emerge from users who feel encumbered by the policy and who don't recognise the reasons behind it. A common example of this may be surfing the Internet. Users who want unfettered access may be tempted to use a modem for direct access to the Internet, thereby circumventing perimeter security measures such as firewalls (which are an absolute must for external defence). Hackers can come down this modem line using a technique known as 'pole-vaulting', and gain all the privileges associated with the device that has the modem attached to it. It should also go without saying that modem numbers should be well protected and not distributed.

A policy is only useful when properly understood by everyone and when enforced rigorously. To do this managers must be able to see any contraventions easily and be able to evidence them so that appropriate action may be taken.

The victimless crime?

One of the challenges with computer security is the idea that it is a victimless crime. If an internal hacker copies a database of customer details, the company still has the database and therefore they may not see it as a crime. It is, however, and the victims are all the people who suffer as a consequence should business levels drop off because a competitor has their customer information.

People often do not realise the financial impact of the time spent to rebuild systems after a vandal has destroyed data, or the loss in service to customers. It all has an impact, and we have a duty to minimise the opportunities for these types of incidents.

We invest in burglar and car alarms. We generally understand physical security because we can see and touch it; but data is often overlooked until it is too late. Try throwing away your computer and what do you miss – the machine or the information on it? We do not leave the keys to the building, the managing director's office and the filing cabinet on a hook by the door, and corporate data should be treated with the same, if not more, sensitivity.

Board responsibilities

There are now a whole host of legal and regulatory requirements detailing the responsibilities of the board or a business owner to ensure that information stored on computers, particularly personal information, is protected from improper use or access.

These include:

■ The Data Protection Act 1998;
■ The Human Rights Act 1998;
■ The E-commerce Directive;
■ The Unfair Contract Terms Act 1977;
■ The Regulation of Investigatory Powers Act 2000;
■ The Electronic Communication Act 2000.

The Turnbull Report, issued in 1999, provides a framework to help interpret the 'Combined Code on Corporate Governance', which is appended to the Listing Rules of the UK Listing Authority. Companies listed on the London Stock Exchange must show that they have assessed the risks to the organisation and that policies are in place to ensure that, as far as is practicable, the potential for damage or loss has been reduced to realistic levels. Although directed at listed companies, the findings of the Turnbull Report are equally applicable to, and make business sense for, other organisations.

The report states that 'the board of directors is responsible for the company's system of internal control. It should set appropriate policies on internal control and seek regular assurance that will enable it to satisfy itself that the system is functioning effectively. It should ensure that the system of internal control is effective in managing those risks in the manner which it has approved'.[1]

Dependence on IT for many firms means that the financial consequences of any loss of information or breach in security should be considered. This needs to be reviewed not simply in terms of the information itself, but also for the cost of preventing further failures and the impact on the company's reputation, brand value, performance and future potential.

---

[1] More at www.icaew.co.uk/internalcontrol

BS 7799 (ISO 17799)

The British Standards Institute (BSI) has published the standard for an Information Security Management System that offers external audit and certification to a recognised British standard, and many organisations are now looking to this as a benchmark for good practice and as a measure of those with whom they wish to trade electronically. This provides an excellent framework for the establishment of the policies and procedures that will allow organisations to protect themselves from security threats, both internal and external, but it also provides a structured manner and common measure for all organisations.

Although formal take-up through the externally audited certification route has been slow, the pace is now quickening with the UK Government mandating compliance across departments and government tenders now making statements about preferred bidders being compliant. When taken in conjunction with the legal aspects of information security, the Turnbull Report and the growing nervousness of the insurance market, BS 7799 and information security management are certainly going to enter the boardroom agenda in the coming months.

A final word on security

Management systems must be put in place and a series of checks and reporting methods established. At the very least a clear and unequivocal security policy should be put in place and staff should be trained to understand its relevance and its requirements. Some of the harm arises from people failing to recognise the value of the data, as pointed out in the 2002 DTI survey that estimates a cost to UK business of some £18 billion per annum.

In general, behaviour is the only way in which we can spot potential data thieves or vandals before the event occurs. This is down to good and sensitive management, and an awareness of staff abilities, life issues and work patterns is essential. Any change in these could be a trigger for such an event.

Monitoring the overall behaviour of people and watching changing patterns of work is also a good way of establishing potential weaknesses. Who is in the office when no one else is – early in the morning or late at night? Is it conscientious work on your behalf or theirs?

We should not, however, be paranoid about people on a personal basis. Most people should understand that your organisation has a security policy and that it is enforced. Equally, it is useless to set a policy if you have no intention of enforcing it, and it is unfair on managers to expect them to implement one without giving them the tools for the job. Once it is understood that the policy is in place and that the tools are there to protect systems and give managers any forensics they may need, all but the most determined data thief/vandal will be put off.

There is no such thing as the perfect system. There is no bank that cannot be robbed, only those that are so strongly protected that softer targets are chosen instead. Security is provided not by one device but by a range of devices, systems and management procedures, built up in layers like the skin of an onion. The outer skins may get damaged, but the inner core is preserved.

There are lessons to be learnt from the disaster recovery business, where corporations have had major fires that destroyed their core assets. Because their corporate information was secure and they had systems in place they were able to continue, unlike those who didn't and perished.

Capitalising on over 20 years experience developing some of the communications protocols at the heart of every Microsoft Windows communications platform, Security Designers Ltd is a privately owned, independent UK-based software company. Emanating from connectivity specialists Network Designers, Security Designers was set up in 2000 to sell and market the award winning Active Net Steward Security Information Management System (SIM) and now has a growing base of UK government, NHS, education and commercial sector organisations, and is quickly establishing a reputation as a leading supplier in the field.

For more information contact: Security Designers Ltd, 5 Wharfe Mews, Cliffe Terrace, Wetherby, Leeds, West Yorkshire LS22 6LX. Tel: +44 (0) 1937 584 584; Fax: +44 (0) 1937 587 367; Email: info@SecurityDesigners.com; Website: www.SecurityDesigners.com

Cyberliabilities in the workplace

Richard Woudberg, legal counsel at Integralis, looks at the balance between freedom and control in the electronic workplace.

The rise in electronic methods of communication such as email and the Internet have provided employees with a greater degree of flexibility and freedom. However, employers wish, and indeed are often compelled by legislation, to maintain control over their employees, and the means by which they can do so can be increasingly intrusive. The need to strike a balance between the concerns of employers and employees is reflected in recent legislation.

Employers have good reason to be concerned about email or Internet usage. Time spent on non-business-related emails or surfing the Internet may reduce profitability by reducing time spent on legitimate business. A recent survey by Websense highlighted that three-quarters of UK companies have dealt with cases of Internet misuse at some point, whilst a survey by Datamonitor has shown that two-thirds of companies are now actively monitoring employee Internet usage.

Some companies have created official policies on employee use of the Internet, informing employees that they may be monitored and expressly barring employees from downloading offensive material. Others have no official policy and actively encourage employees to go online as much as possible to gain insight on competitors and customers.

Employers may risk being vicariously liable for defamatory material communicated by email. In a high profile case of recent years, incorrect rumours concerning a rival insurance company were circulated on Norwich Union's internal email system, with the result that Norwich Union paid out nearly half a million pounds in a court settlement to the rival company.

As email is so quick and easy, there is an increased risk that employees may unwittingly enter into contracts that bind their employers. A disclaimer should therefore be included on all emails that are sent out.

Use of email also brings an increased risk of leakage of confidential information, which may be an employer's business secrets, or confidential employee information. Employers should include in their electronic communications policy a clause to the effect that no confidential information is to be sent via email or that if it is, it must be encrypted. Additionally, the use of encrypted emails must also be monitored, as it is a mechanism by which confidential information can leave an organisation without being interrogated for inappropriate content.

Furthermore employers now have a duty under the Data Protection Act (DPA) 1998 to prevent unauthorised access to employee information and must therefore take adequate security measures to comply with this.

Employers will also be concerned to prevent the infection of their networks by viruses, which may enter the system via attachments to emails sent from outside. 'Spam' (unsolicited or junk email) uses valuable bandwidth and email server space and wastes email recipients' time. Spoof email can deceive the recipient into clicking on a hyperlink that connects to a prohibited site and can even request information to be returned by 'reply to sender' command, which can have disastrous consequences in terms of data-loss of trade secrets, betrayal of client confidentiality or theft of data.

An employer may be vicariously liable if its employees create a working atmosphere that gives rise to sexual or racial harassment claims by other employees. Employees might do this by downloading or sending to other employees emails which that employee considers offensive, such as sexually explicit jokes. Liability for such claims is not subject to any cap and such claims can be costly.

Directors or other appropriate officers of a company may be liable if their employees send obscene material by way of email. Under the Telecommunications Terminal Equipment Regulations 1992 an employee may be found guilty of an offence if he/she sends material that is grossly offensive or of an indecent, obscene or menacing character by means of a public telecommunication system. If the employer is a company, then the company's officers may also be guilty of an offence if they are found to have consented to the above, or simply to have neglected to restrain the employee from his or her actions.

In the event of a dispute between employer and employee, emails may provide vital evidence, but such evidence would be disallowed by the court or tribunal if it has been obtained unlawfully.

Controlling employee use of electronic communications

There is an increasing range of products now available that can monitor email and Internet use by employees. Email content can be checked by keyword to filter out any that contain specified words, for example the phrase 'business plan' might be used to target employees engaging in rival business activities. Even more sophisticated products are available that are set up to monitor the overall context of communications rather than focusing on keywords.

Internet use may be monitored by recording websites visited and time spent on each, and employers can prevent access to certain websites by installing software that blocks access to a database of sites that they control. For example, it is possible to classify types of site – ie business/non-business sites – and use this to stop employees accessing pornographic sites on the Internet.

Avoiding monitoring problems

Employers should have a clear policy on the use of communications, which includes guidance on Internet sites to avoid and on the appropriate use of email and the telephone. For example, a company might allow a certain amount of personal use of email and the telephone but not allow personal use of the Internet, and this should be made clear in the policy.

Notably, the DPA draft code states that with regard to Internet use, where the main concern for employers is the accessing and downloading of pornographic material, the statement that 'pornographic' sites are prohibited is not clear enough. Interestingly, the code also queries whether directors would be likely to be held liable for their employees sending obscene material by email if such use was clearly prohibited. It should be borne in mind of course that employees may inadvertently access prohibited sites, for example by clicking on a hyperlink in a spoof email or through a search facility.

The policy should warn employees that their emails may be monitored, highlight the disciplinary sanctions for inappropriate use of email or the Internet, and be included in the employment contracts and company handbook. It is also advisable to put a message on computer screens stating that the computer user consents to monitoring as stated in the company handbook.

The DPA draft code states that in ascertaining an employee's expectations or otherwise of privacy, regard will be had to the monitoring that takes place in practice rather than to the policy, so that if no monitoring takes place in practice, then it is not legitimate to suddenly start monitoring.

Employees should be consulted on the benefits of an Internet policy to ensure that the employer's conduct is seen as reasonable. The existence of a policy that is communicated to employees may be enough to allow employers to monitor without fear of redress from employees. Nevertheless, it may be desirable to go further and provide a separate computer terminal that is stated to be private, and likewise a separate telephone.

Oftel has published guidance on what should be included in a telephone use policy, including the approved nature and timing of personal calls and disciplinary measures for flouting the policy. It states that warnings alone may not be enough to counteract the 'legitimate expectation of privacy', and that separate phone lines should be provided for private calls. It also suggests that monitoring should be confined to that which is 'necessary and proportionate' to the issue it is seeking to address – for example, by using an itemised record of phone calls to find out about misuse of the phone by employees rather than by recording calls, which is more intrusive.

For monitoring to be fair in terms of the code, the impact on the employee and his/her rights to a reasonable degree of privacy should be considered. The code states that the risks to be dealt with and benefits obtained by monitoring should be proportionate to the effects on the employee. Monitoring should be targeted to those employees who present a risk, and it is important to be aware of the specific business purpose for which the monitoring is to be carried out.

Monitoring, states the code, should be as unobtrusive as possible in order to attain the business objective. This can be achieved by itemising calls rather than listening to the content; by using spot checks rather than continuously monitoring; by using automated methods where possible; and by monitoring the traffic of data rather than the content.

Where emails are accessed when staff are away, emails that are clearly personal should not be opened. In this regard it would be helpful if employees were told to keep personal and business emails separate.

Another very important concern for employers will be the effect the new legislation may have on the use of email evidence by employers in tribunal claims. Emails often provide a very useful evidential trail, but evidence gathered by email monitoring that has been obtained in contravention of the Regulation of Investigatory Powers (RIP) Act or the Human Rights Act will be inadmissible.

Integralis, the corporate solutions division of Articon-Integralis, provides information security solutions to all industry sectors throughout the world, allowing organisations to grow and achieve their business goals securely. These solutions combine services and system integration, the deployment of 'best-of-breed' security products, as well as managed security services, and employ some of the leading technologists and most skilled engineers in the industry. Integralis is recognised as a leading and trusted provider of information security solutions in the European IT and e-commerce security market. For further information contact: Integralis Ltd, Theale House, Brunel Road, Theale, Reading, RG7 4AQ. Tel: +44(0)1189 306060; Fax: +44(0)1189 302143.
Email: info@integralis.co.uk; Website: www.integralis.co.uk

Data complacency

Is the proliferation of information fostering a dangerous shift in corporate mentality? Humphrey Browning, Head of Technical Consultancy at Nexor, looks at how networks can inadvertently lead to mismanaged data and under-valued information.

According to a report by Jupiter Research,[1] 49.5 per cent of CIOs (chief information officers) considered the sensitivity of their company's data as 'low'. In a world where the threat of information security breaches is an everyday consideration, this either represents gross naivety or complete negligence. The sad reality is that by opening up networks and building knowledge-based infrastructures that empower employees to access a wider port-folio of corporate information, organisations have inadvertently opened the floodgates for mismanaged data and fostered a climate of undervalued information.

Technologies such as email pose a potentially dangerous shift in corporate mentality, a shift that is seeing the sensitivity of corporate data increasingly undermined through an ability to circulate information with a degree of immediacy that was unthinkable just a few years ago. Sensitive company documents, which would once have been physically filed, marked as confidential and sealed in an envelope when sent to an external party, are now easily accessible from a corporate network by large numbers of employees who have the means at hand to routinely circulate its contents around the world without a second thought.

Whilst a great deal of attention is given to the security of data that pass the perimeter of an enterprise, many organisations have been unsuccessful in managing the root data itself. The growing volume of material held within the average company is now so large that,

---

[1] Jupiter Executive Survey, July 2001

although freely available through company intranets and directories, its level of confidentiality is often left uncategorised. It is this unchallenged availability and the ease with which it can be circulated by an employee with an email connection that is presenting a security risk that has so far largely gone unnoticed. In most cases the circulation of sensitive data, perhaps a sales forecast or share price information, is not conducted maliciously. Instead it is carried out by the growing army of employees to whom email is second nature, who perhaps don't assign as much importance to a piece of data as their contemporaries would have done ten years ago.

For centuries technology has been the root cause of changes within business practice. The telephone, fax and PC are all typical modern examples of how, once accepted as mainstream, technology can lead us along a new path of increased profitability, efficiency and communication. In the majority of cases such changes are welcomed, and this is certainly the case with email, a technology adopted with such speed and ferocity that to anyone under the age of 21 it seems hard to imagine life without it.

The problem is compounded by the rise in information security breaches, the reaction to which of many organisations is to batten down the hatches and ring fence corporate networks with the latest software solutions. Yet, despite these measures, many organisations continue to allow themselves to be easy prey by not offering a second thought to the unclassified material attached to their emails.

Of course, the suggestion is not to restrict email access across an enterprise; the advent of electronic communication certainly offers more benefits than pitfalls. Not only have previously mundane work processes been simplified, but employees also have a far wider perspective of understanding thanks to the availability of data that would have once been locked away in a filing cabinet. Knowledge workers must be allowed to search, retrieve and manage both data and email within a secure, yet collaborative, environment.

Many email solution vendors have been slow to recognise the growing demands placed on email as a business tool, undoubtedly fertilising the trend towards free information flow whatever the cost. It should be remembered that email was never intended to be used as a tool for high-value communication. Only when it became a viable mass-market technology did it begin to flourish in industries where the confidentiality of information is critical to business. Efforts to secure data circulated by email have largely been pooled around encryption technologies, yet the problem lies further down the chain, at the root source of unmanaged company information.

The way in which organisations are conducting business highlights the need to automatically classify email content in its native form from within a corporate directory based on defined rules of usage that are unique to each organisation. Policies and controls should be put in place to ensure the security of sensitive information without restricting its accessibility within an organisation. Wrapping low-level data, such as company phone lists or staff memos, in security mechanisms achieves nothing but to restrict accessibility and use.

One sector that has long understood the importance of classifying information is the military. Using security labelling technology, electronic communications are 'tagged' before dispatch. The security labels, usually applied within the default email client, allow the sender to quickly assign a level of confidentiality suitable to a particular mail and its contents. The label then automatically applies the appropriate level of security for the level of confidentiality selected.

An email of the highest confidentiality will therefore be subject to digital signing, data encryption and any other mechanism that is in place to guarantee the integrity of the data. A staff memo, depending on its content, may in turn pass through the gateway untouched.

Security labelling is now being applied within the corporate environment, with a new generation of software adopting a more pragmatic approach by managing email on the boundary between organisations and the outside world. This approach offers the benefits of configurable policy-setting at a server level, allowing the definition and management of email policies from a corporate perspective regardless of desktop set-up. The responsibility for applying security is thus removed from the user and passed back to the organisation.

It seems it is not only the information that is undervalued, but also the resulting effects of mismanaged data and the possibility of a breach in confidentiality. Online IT resource centre TechRepublic conducted a survey in January 2002[2] in which nearly 2,000 respondents were questioned about email and Internet usage. Surprisingly, only 18 per cent of those questioned considered the leakage of company confidential information as 'extremely serious', with respondents citing employees accessing pornographic content via the Internet or email as more of a threat. Unbelievably, just nine per cent felt that the problem was 'serious', less than half the number that cited the serious nature of downloading unauthorised files such as MP3s.

The same survey also looked at organisations that had fired employees on the grounds of Internet or email misuse. Again, the leakage of confidential material appeared low amongst the grounds for dismissal. Dismissals for recreational Internet surfing in work time (26 per cent of firings) were more than double those for leaking company confidential data (10 per cent). This represents one of two things: either organisations place a lower importance on a breach of confidentiality than on recreational surfing, which is unlikely, or they do not have the tools in place to either detect or prevent such information misuse. In fact, according to the DTI's *Information Security Breaches Survey 2002*, only 27 per cent of companies have a documented security policy.

As more and more organisations become dependent on both electronic communication and electronic data and retrieval systems, the potential for security breaches will undoubtedly increase, no matter how much investment is made into perimeter security or user authentication solutions.

The age-old adage that the weakest link in any electronic network is the user holds true. Organisations must look internally at how employees are trained to use information and also create an understanding that corporate data is an asset and not a by-product of modern business. There is a strong argument that responsibility for security and confidentiality of information must be moved away from the user and managed centrally without, of course, restricting access. Unlike many other threats to electronic communication, this problem is entirely preventable and lies solely at the feet of an army of email users who unwittingly show complacency to valuable information each time they access their email accounts.

---

[2] Results of survey are available from www.techrepublic.com

Humphrey Browning is Head of Technical Consultancy at Nexor. Nexor provides high-assurance messaging and directory solutions to government, military, finance and telecommunications markets. Nexor customers can be found in Europe, North America, Canada and Australia, and cover a range of commercial and military organisations. The US Army, CIA, NSA, Canadian DoD and Government of Canada all utilise Nexor technology, as do the UK MoD, GCHQ and armed forces.

For further information contact: European Office (Headquarters), Nexor Limited, Rutherford House, Nottingham Science & Technology Park, Nottingham NG7 2PZ, UK. Tel: +44 (0)115 952 0500; Fax: +44 (0)115 952 0519; Email: info@nexor.com

The marketing dimension

Information security can be both an enabler and a destroyer of value, writes Michael Harrison, Chairman of Harrison Smith Associates.

What 'marketing aspects'?

Marketing surrounding the 'e-world' should be simple – everyone will utilise 'e', therefore turn your communications to directing prospects and clients to the appropriate website, and to your email address, and carry on. Why bother about marketing the methodology? Why not stick to marketing your products? 'Business as usual – just faster and more responsive', should be the cry. No problem there for the marketing manager? Perhaps – and perhaps not.

The trouble with our new 'e'- communicating society is that it gives us new tools that provide immense power to the user. Why is that a trouble? Because of the word 'user', which is not to be confused with the word 'owner'. This is a new concept and it has not been fully understood even by those who claim to be 'experts', because they are 'IT specialists' and this is (or should be) a senior management rather than a technical issue.

Unless we take proper measures anyone can become the 'user', without the 'owner' knowing. Most of us have computers. We feel that we 'own' our PC – even if our organisations actually paid for them – but unless proper measures are taken we may well be sharing 'usership' with others. Either they know everything that we do, or they use part of 'our' computer's power for their purposes; or they come in and alter our information, or are totally destructive, or act 'merely' as vandals.

Suddenly the marketing manager is looking rather vulnerable, because his/her organisation is vulnerable, and the fallout will be lack of trust and reputation, which leads to brand problems. We all know that good brand reputation is difficult to create, easy to damage, and much more difficult to repair once it is damaged. And today, damage is far easier to create. Why? In the 'old days' when we obtained a new technology, a 'new tool to help our business', it was *ours* to play with – we made the decision about when, if and how to use it. There was no thought that it could bite the hand that bought it. We owned it, we used it, we made the decisions. There was nothing else to say.

Equally, in the 'old days' (and remember, many organisations are still in these 'old days') we believed that 'an Englishman's home (business) is his castle'. So we guarded our perimeter like mad – we had locks, bolts, fences, guards, alarm systems, etc – and as long as the perimeter was not breached we felt 'safe'.

Okay, there was always the challenge of the odd rogue member of staff, and the 'temp' (or the cleaner, or whoever) who was not exactly what they were supposed to be, but, by and large, we felt secure from external attack, and an insider still had to take the information out of the premises physically, and was thus vulnerable.

And if by chance we did find someone 'up to something', it was nice and clear and they could be sacked, whether or not we pressed charges. Of course security was important, but it was physical security that worried us – and the police were always there to back us up if our physical perimeter was breached.

So what had this to do with marketing? In those days, almost nothing – security was seldom used as a differentiator. If you were handling cash, or high-value items, or drugs or anything with a high 'street value', then it was presumed that you had put in the necessary security.

'Safe as the Bank of England' was a saying from the past – and more recently there have been advertising campaigns that talk about getting the security of certain groups of companies 'around you'. Physical security plus financial security – something you could kick and feel and see – providing a nice warm feeling.

You were pretty clear about whether or not your organisation was a 'target'. You could identify your physical defences and contrast them with the value that an attacker might steal (such as cash, valuables and easily disposable items), or you could decide you were just not worth attacking! In retrospect, a nice, simple life.

So marketing in general took security for granted, and certainly did not get directly involved. And please note that 'security' meant one thing only: protection from actual physical loss. Therefore, the items were being protected from being stolen, copied or destroyed. But who thought of protecting things from being altered? Or from being kept out of your own reach for a crucial period of time?

Also, most items were 'physical'. Yes of course documents were often involved, especially if they had intrinsic value, but the protection of information was rarely discussed because information was not such a readily available commodity. Today, the 'e-revolution' has broken through our parameters. A modern organisation that communicates by email and via the Internet has inserted the equivalent of the M25 straight into itself – and anything can drive along it, unless you have taken the necessary management decisions followed by the necessary technical responses.

It is never the other way round: you have to take the information risk management decisions at board level, and then inform the IT department of the criteria against which to work. It is madness to expect the IT people to understand the relative value of each type of information within your organisation and its relative importance in terms of confidentiality, integrity and availability. So what does all this mean for today's marketing management?

These marketing aspects!

You are responsible (on behalf of your board) for the protection and enhancement of your brand. Almost everything stems from that responsibility, because if you allow your brand to be damaged then everything else suffers, and the spiral is downwards, fast!

Pre-'e' your brand was similarly affected by your reputation. Nothing new there then; except that today someone can affect your reputation (and your brand) from the other side of the world, without actually caring one jot about what they are doing, and at almost zero cost to themselves either in time, resources or actual financial outlay.

What is worse, they often do not realise what they are doing to you – they do not understand the consequences of their actions. It is almost as if a baby has been given the controls to a guided-weapons system – it has no concept of what it is doing when it presses the buttons, but the result is as catastrophic as it would be if 'an expert' did it deliberately.

It is too easy to do damage electronically, and it is made too easy by the very fact that we rely on communicating by a system that was never designed to be secure. The Internet was originally built to allow communication amongst academic groups, known for their preference for sharing information. It was not supposed to be the world's 'trusted business backbone'.

The other reason why it is too easy to create 'electronic damage' is that too many organisations and individuals do not understand why they must take steps to protect their 'e'-base. They think (if they think about it at all) that it is 'someone else's responsibility'. It is seen as a technological issue – even by managers who should know better.

Thus, we have a new challenge: the owners of information do not control access to it, whereas the access controllers (the IT management) do not know the relative value and vulnerability of the different types of information flowing round their networks.

Still, there is one overriding issue that is obvious: our most valuable asset today is information. With it we can continue our businesses whatever disasters may happen, whereas without it we are floundering like fish out of water. Therefore it is our information that we must protect, remembering that 'information' includes details of every aspect of our organisation, from what we produce, how we produce it (and what we buy to produce it) to why we produce it, details of to whom we sell it and through what channels, at what prices, and using which staff – everything. It is our human resources information, it is our future plans, our patents pending, our next acquisition, our commercial documentation, our websites, our manufacturing settings, our quality controls, our marketing databases… and it is all 'online', unless we have made very careful decisions about how we manage it.

So we can have the equivalent of our Crown Jewels being unprotected on the equivalent of the M25 in our organisation, and yet we can have 'virtual armed guards' protecting something that is in the public domain anyway. It is easy for this to happen, particularly if there is a lack of understanding and communication between IT and the rest of the organisation (especially marketing).

Shouldn't marketing be responsible for such communication? Are we not responsible for everything that can affect the brand? The answer has to be yes; so another marketing aspect of the new 'e-world' is that marketing itself must take responsibility for all of these communications.

Trust and confidence affect brands, and marketing has responsibility for the brand. Therefore marketing has direct responsibility for ensuring that your organisation promotes and ensures 'e-trust' and 'e-confidence'. Furthermore, marketing must also take responsibility for all internal and external communications on this issue, otherwise they will occur in a piecemeal fashion, undertaken by people who are not trained in communications skills.

The expectation: experience equation

Whatever we do, we cannot claim to have 'e-trust' and 'e-confidence' unless we have genuinely got it. Remember that many so-called 'hackers' carry out attacks just to be able to say that they have got through a specific organisation's defences. You may claim to be secure – they may well try you out!

To have an Information Security (Assurance) Management System (ISMS or IAMS) in place and working properly will provide you with the assurance that you require to make such a claim in the first place. But that is not the reason to have such a system – you need it in order to conduct business electronically, whether you go public about having it or not.

So the answer to the question 'do we publicise our security, or do we keep quiet about it' matters not; you need it to carry out business, even if you only intend to tell your stakeholders (clients, suppliers and staff included).

But what can happen?

Viruses, worms, trojans, deliberate attacks (external hackers, internal hackers, recent leaver-hackers, hactivists), random attacks from the same communities and errors (as all the above can be 'let in' by mistake) and, in addition, simple human error can, in a poorly protected system, wreak havoc.

The cost in terms of economic damage from the above sources for just the first 9 months of 2002 is estimated to be between US$32 –39 billion for overt digital attacks only – not including the errors.

And just in case you are saying to yourself, 'Okay, but I am/we are not likely to be targets' (which totally ignores the random nature of viruses etc and the potential for internal attacks), let us look at some actual examples.

1. The 'mistake' (or 'I didn't mean to destroy your livelihood')

Recently a 'hactivist' (someone who believes that their hacking is 'ethical' because they only break into sites and systems that are owned or run by organisations that they don't agree with) destroyed a company that was totally innocent, even of the so-called 'crime' that the hactivist was so worked-up about.

Unfortunately for the company its original founder had chosen a name that was similar to the name of a business that was connected with the use of animals for their fur – not the same name; not the target name; and the business certainly had nothing to do with the practice so hated by the hactivist. The company was totally innocent – and is now totally out of business.

A 'simple case of mistaken identity' was how it was portrayed, but the end result was catastrophic for the owners and all of the workers, simply because someone who was so full of their own 'rights' made an electronic search for any company that had a similar name and attacked them without any further check.

2. The 'game' ('I wanted to prove that I could "take someone out"')

Even more recently an Internet Service Provider (ISP) – not exactly an organisation without 'e'-technical nous – suffered a total 'distributed denial of service' attack. This meant that none of their customers could use their services for over a week – they went out of business as a direct result.

3. The 'idiot' (or someone who thinks that they are 'above all of this')

A large IT company had a very costly virus attack; despite the fact that it prides itself on assisting many areas of 'UK plc' to solve technology challenges. How could anything get past its sophisticated protection systems?

Simple: the CEO did not believe that the rules applied to them, and brought in a disk created on their son's home PC – complete with a highly unpleasant virus. Due to an earlier mistake the virus was 'inside' their firewall – and made hay! The cost was well over £10,000,000, just to their internal systems.

4. The 'good idea' (or 'let's do this using "e"' – without thinking)

A company offered free internet advertising to clients of another service. Someone 'hacked in' and changed the prices shown. Apart from the nightmare of sorting it all out, the reputation of the company was badly shaken when the object of the exercise was the complete opposite!

5. The 'unhappy employee' (either as a cause or as a victim)

Consider two scenarios. The first involved a person who saw a pornographic scene on another employee's PC screen. They sued the company, and won considerable damages – nearly into six figures – for sexual harassment.

The second involved someone who was, appropriately, fired from their job. Their employer was excellent in providing new employees with passwords etc – but not at all good at removing them when people left, even in bad circumstances. The ex-employee decided to 'get even' and logged into the company system using their old password, and altered many detailed items in areas such as personnel records, payroll, and costing and pricing.

The trouble was that no one knew exactly where that person had accessed, and the cost of redressing the 'vandalism' was measured in man-years.

The marketing effects? The costs were considerable, not only with their existing clients and prospects but also in the job market where the company gained a poor HR reputation.

Summary

It is marketing's job to control communication about information security, inside and outside the organisation. A company's approach to security will directly affect its marketing positioning and organisational differentiation. Security failure can destroy a company's reputation – or even the company itself.

Information security is not a cost, it is a marketing investment. Everyone is a potential target and you cannot afford to ignore this subject. E-business and e-government demand the electronic exchange of ever-more important information.

Marketing should identify and promote the internal and external advantages of having appropriate information security. It should work with IT to achieve a perceived 'trusted status', and take responsibility for creating detailed positioning and differentiation messages.

Marketing should create two communications plans: one internal, one external. Finally, marketing must ensure that all communications are written in suitable language for each target audience – internal and external – otherwise the messages will not be understood.

Michael Harrison Dip.M., F.C.I.M. is Chairman of Harrison Smith Associates Limited and Chairman, UK, of the 'Protecting Critical Information Infrastructures Initiative'. For further information contact: Michael R Harrison, Chairman, Harrison Smith Associates Ltd, Third Floor, Diamond House, 36–38 Hatton Garden, London EC1N 8EB. Tel: +44 (0)20 7404 5444; Fax: +44 (0)20 7404 8222; Website: www.hsaltd.co.uk

Stamping out the bugs

Tony Neate has spent a total of 27 years as a detective, 13 years of this working in commercial fraud and eight years in computer crime, so he knows all about crime – cybercrime and other forms. He is the Industry Liaison Officer at the NHTCU and the fact that he has such extensive experience demonstrates how much importance the unit places on its relationship with business.

The NHTCU, which became operational in October 2001, has a multi-agency approach to tackling problems raised by the use of computers and the Internet for criminal activity of various types.

The unit, based in Docklands, East London, is headed by Detective Chief Superintendent Len Hynds, a career detective from the National Crime Squad. The unit comprises representatives from the National Crime Squad, The National Crime Intelligence Service (NCIS), HM Customs & Excise and the Military. It also has strong links with Computer Crime Units (CCUs) in all police forces throughout the UK and with other law enforcement agencies across the country.

The NHTCU conducts operations at national and international levels. It has responsibility for making strategic assessments and developing intelligence; supporting local law enforcement with advice and co-ordination; developing best advice for law enforcement and business practice on computer crime prevention. It also liaises closely with the IT industry, including Internet Service Providers (ISPs), telecommunications companies and software houses.

Tony Neate says: 'The aim of the NHTCU is to assist in the policing of cyber-crime nationally and transnationally, and to add to the capabilities already existing at a local level. By its very nature cybercrime does not recognise national borders. It is a global problem and needs a global solution. The NHTCU is just one part of the joined-up approach being taken by the police around the world that has been necessary to deal with its unique new crime.

'The idea is to create a partnership between law enforcement and industry. We can provide industry with strategic and practical intelligence examples of attacks so that they are aware of the problems and can put the necessary policies and hardware in place. What we do we do together, not alone. We want to make business aware that there is highly capable expertise locally, and on top of that there are well-trained officers, who are experts in dealing with serious and organised crime, that have turned their attentions to hi-tech attacks. We deal with incidents sympathetically, in partnership, and in a way whereby the businesses do not lose control.'

Computers and the Internet present great benefits to society. However they also present opportunities for crime, much of it simply conventional crime using new technology. Computer crime takes many forms and is grouped into two broad types of activity: existing offences that can become more complicated to prevent and detect with new technology; and new offences that can only be committed with the use of such technology. As Tony says, 'Anything that can happen in the real world can happen in the cyberworld – theft, deception, extortion, whatever.'

Cybercrime covers fraud of many types – hacking, industrial espionage, 'viruses' and 'denial of service', organised paedophilia, intellectual property theft (ie the illicit copying of video, other recordings and software), money laundering and crimes of violence such as kidnap.

Tony says: 'Viruses are the scourge of business. Time is paramount to most businesses; when a virus attaches itself to a company's critical system, the system can be taken down for hours or even days. "Denial of service" attacks can lead to major extortion demands.' In order to explain the nature of a denial of service attack, Tony uses the delivery of a traditional letter by way of example. 'A postman may deliver two or three letters a day; similarly with emails, you might expect several a day. But can you imagine what would happen if your postman delivered millions of letters to your postbox every second. You wouldn't be able to move; and similarly with a denial of service attack, millions of pieces of data being received by your computer in seconds would very quickly use up all your available bandwidth and you can't do business.'

Part of the problem for business is that many are aware of cybercrime, which may put them off embarking on an e-commerce strategy. But if businesses are aware of the problems they can profit as long as they put the right safeguards in place. 'Businesses need to be aware of the problems. One part of a simple strategy is setting up firewalls. A simple firewall, properly configured, can cost as little as £50–60; for far bigger businesses, an intrusion detection system may cost thousands of pounds – it really is horses for courses.'

And it is not just about dealing with the threat from outside. Companies also need to look inside, to internal threats from employees. 'It is important that employees are aware of the company's policies and procedures and that the contracts of employment clearly state what these are. Companies need to put security protocols and emergency responses in place. Employers must also keep up with the new and changing laws and regulations in this area, so that they are aware of their responsibilities.'

Of course one of the problems with cybercrime and how it affects business is that quite often, due to commercial sensitivities, businesses do not want word getting out that they have been hit. The NHTCU is sympathetic to these concerns and has put in place a confidential reporting system and is prepared to enter into a non-disclosure agreement. 'We want to build up trust, but that trust will take time. We are fully aware that if we break that trust then industry will lose all confidence in us.' It is for this reason that Tony couldn't provide any good-news stories on how the unit had worked with industry in this way, but did say that the fact that he couldn't was in itself good news. What he could say was that they were working closely with all sectors of industry – manufacturing, services, finance and transportation – and that within those sectors the NHTCU have helped a number of businesses.

To find out more about the National Hi-Tech Crime Unit see www.nhtcu.org or contact Tony Neate, Industry Liaison Officer at admin@nhtcu.org.

2

Points of exposure

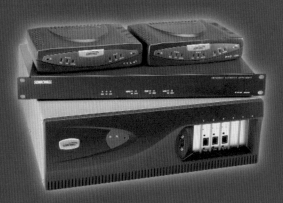

Email

There is a gaping hole in every organisation that exposes them to untold risk: email. Indicii Salus reports on the dangers of unprotected emails and reviews how best to safeguard their confidentiality, integrity and authenticity.

Email is one of the most simple and effective communication tools available. It is quick, convenient and cheap, but unless used properly, fundamentally insecure. It is as public as a postcard and leaves a written record long after it has been erased, meaning that any skilled or knowledgeable person can recover a long-forgotten or buried email message from deep inside a networked system. There is no doubt that in a business environment the use of email and the Internet poses a threat to a business's ability to protect company intellectual property and other confidential information.

The Office for National Statistics' *Internet Access* report (2002) demonstrated that, for UK users, email was one of the Internet's most widely used and valuable applications, with 71 per cent of users accessing email on a regular basis.[1] The overwhelming majority of those users, however, fail to adequately protect their email system from possible attacks.

In an article published in May 1999 by BBC News Online, it was reported that research group Information Data Services (IDS) had urged employers to draw up clear 'cyber-liability' policies in the wake of several high-profile industrial tribunals on the use of electronic media at work. It is clear that the government needs to set out definite guidelines and regulations for the safe use of email. The events of 11 September 2001 brought new challenges to the protection of privacy in the modern age that led governments worldwide to extend control over individuals through the law and technology.

---

[1] 9.7 billion emails were sent in the UK over the last year.

The big question

It is unquestionable that email security is the next big IT security issue – a fact that gives rise to the following question: if a company's most valuable asset apart from its workforce is its intellectual property, why are so many businesses failing to take the crucial steps towards protecting that property in its electronic form when it would be both simple and cost-effective for them to do so?

Given the strictly monitored methods that are applied to the treatment of hard-copy letters and other documents, it is highly illogical for electronically transmitted information to be treated in the haphazard and insecure fashion that typifies common business practice regarding the use of email. There is no truly viable reason why the majority of businesses are failing to take the crucial steps to protect their intellectual property, especially when it is considered that emails have now replaced letters as the most widely used form of business communication in the UK. Emails – *which are as legally binding as paper letters* – need to be signed securely, subject to document controls, delivered safely, protected from interception or intrusion, and generally treated with the same respect as paper-based communications. To treat them in what amounts to an offhand fashion would be asking for trouble.

The main challenge to be met by IT security professionals is to overturn corporate Britain's complacency in the face of clear but avoidable threats to the confidentiality of electronically transmitted information. Support for the IT industry has ultimately come from the government with the implementation of the Data Protection Act (1998) and the BS 7799 standard, which has strong repercussions for anybody wishing to communicate using email.

IT security experts would obviously understand the issues surrounding treatment of the Internet in greater depth than the average man in the street, but the need to extend this awareness to all Internet users is now critical. Letters have been used as a form of communication for thousands of years, so there is no wonder that people have learnt how to deal with them safely. For the Internet – and consequently email – there has been far less time for users to absorb the underlying principles and implications surrounding its use.

Threats to email

The main points of exposure within the process of sending unprotected email are:

1. Confidentiality

The information sent is vulnerable to being anonymously read by any unauthorised person whilst in transit. Hack-attacks of this kind are very easy to perform by almost anyone who has the will to do so. *A good analogy for this type of email hack is the postman who allows another person to read other people's postcards before delivering them to the rightful recipients.*

2. Integrity

The contents of an unprotected email can also be anonymously modified while they are in transit and then passed onto the recipient as if they were the original message, without either the recipient or sender being any the wiser. *As an extension of the analogy given in point 1 above, an individual could forge alterations to the postcard before allowing it to be delivered by the postman.*

3. Authenticity

Emails can be easily and anonymously forged so that messages appear to be from a certain person. These could then be sent to somebody without either the person whose name was forged or the recipient ever discovering that the message was not genuine. This form of hacking is known as spoofing. *In this case a forger would write and sign a postcard in somebody else's name before sending it to the chosen victim.*

Consequences

Cyber-criminals – and it is known that the majority of them operate covertly *within their own company* – go about their business for a variety of reasons. These range from an intention to gain a competitive edge (corporate espionage) to the desire to exact revenge or to further a political cause. It is painfully simple for an employee to check the emails of another employee and it should come as no surprise that, according to current research,[2] over 70 per cent of IT security breaches are committed by an organisation's own staff, although employers seldom take adequate steps to safeguard their confidential correspondence from internal spies. Whatever the case may be, the consequences are often severe and the majority of victims who have had their email attacked try to cover up the situation for fear of the embarrassment (or other undesirable scenario) that might ensue if the vulnerability were to become publicly known.

There are well-documented cases in the media about what can happen when emails are left lurking unprotected for anybody to unearth, for example, the case of Jo Moore, whose confidential emails to Transport Secretary Stephen Byers were leaked in the wake of 11 September 2001, to the great embarrassment of both herself and the government. Another well-known case happened on 3 November 2000, when an anti-Israeli hacker attacked the website of one of Washington's most powerful lobbying organisations, the American–Israeli Public Affairs Committee (Aipac). The attacker, the self-styled 'Doctor Nuker, founder of the Pakistan Hackerz Club', published critical emails downloaded from Aipac's own databases, as well as credit card numbers and email addresses of Aipac members.

Reasons to address the threats

While horror stories abound, the average business or private user of email might feel they have nothing much to hide and are unlikely targets for hackers. Unfortunately, there is no room for naiveté of this kind:

1. The Data Protection Act (1998) makes it clear that specific steps *must* be taken to secure certain types of information:
2. 'The Act contains eight Data Protection Principles. These state that all data must be:

---

[2] Data from Diligence Information Security.

- processed fairly and lawfully;
- obtained and used only for specified and lawful purposes;
- adequate, relevant and not excessive;
- accurate and, where necessary, kept up to date;
- kept for no longer than necessary;
- processed in accordance with the individual's rights (as defined);
- kept secure;
- transferred only to countries that offer adequate data protection'.[3]

3. Given that emails that have apparently been deleted can still be dredged from the hard drive of a user's PC (and Oliver North would testify to this), it stands to reason that the safe-deletion function offered by email encryption solutions is the most practical method for ensuring that information relating to out-of-date records is properly disposed of.[4]

4. The basic right to privacy is something to which everybody is entitled, but basic rights can be taken for granted until such times as they are forcibly taken away. The ability of hackers to cause chaos is a real and present danger that should not be ignored by anyone, even if they consider their own emails to be totally innocuous. At some stage most Internet users send information by email that they would rather keep as private correspondence between themselves and their chosen recipient; so why would those users chance their credibility or reputation by sending an email in an unprotected format? Recent EU directives on data privacy a urge companies to protect the data that they deal in as it makes its way across cyberspace.

5. BS 7799, first published in February 1995 (revised in May 1999), is a comprehensive set of controls comprising best practices in information security and is meant to serve as a single reference point for identifying the controls needed for most situations where IT systems are used in industry and commerce. The international version of the directive is ISO/IEC 17799: 2000.

These standards constitute the benchmark against which all companies will be measured, and it has been suggested that an organisation's BS 7799 status should be included in its annual returns/annual report.[5] To ignore or contravene the best practice guidelines laid out by BS 7799 and ISO/IEC 17799: 2000 would leave a company open to various liabilities from other laws or from contractual obligations. For example, the unwitting disclosure (because of an unprotected email) of somebody else's trade secret or material given under a non-disclosure agreement (NDA) would be considered gross negligence.

---

[3] This excerpt is background information taken from the Data Protection Act Shop's website at: www.data-protection-act.co.uk.

[4] The overall security of email is likely to be of greater immediate concern to certain types of organisation, especially those in the public sector. The health service, for example, has an urgent need to guarantee the privacy of patient records during communications, and thus has a greater awareness of both the Data Protection Act itself, the risks posed by insecurity, and the methods that can be used to achieve the required level of protection.

[5] Information taken from the www.securityrisk.co.uk website, which provides advice on BS 7799 compliance.

Some people believe that the future of security enforcement lies with insurance and that companies will be liable for damage caused by faulty products or procedures, regardless of any broad disclaimer statements they might have made. Companies would then insure against such claims, and premiums would vary depending on implementation of security features. Enhanced security would, therefore, become not just a legal requirement but also a financial advantage (due to lower insurance premiums).

It is clear that there is a widespread lack of awareness regarding secure emailing practices. In both public and private sectors a security policy is the most basic discipline in information security; but almost 75 per cent of businesses do not have any such clearly defined policy. Only 49 per cent have documented procedures to ensure compliance with the Data Protection Act (1998). As mentioned above, the recognised international standards for information security management are BS 7799 and the related ISO/IEC 17799: 2000, but only 15 per cent of people responsible for IT security are aware of their content.

Reducing the risks and eliminating the threat

Whilst it is true that information security has become a greater priority in the last two years, especially at board level, the threats have also increased substantially. Modern cryptography techniques and services can add substantial benefits to electronic business arrangements. These techniques can scramble data to avoid unauthorised disclosure, and also to ensure the integrity, authenticity and legitimacy of electronic communication records and computerised transactions. Whether or not businesses in the UK actually get this message still remains to be seen.

There are robust, readily available solutions that can be used to protect electronic mail and these usually consist of two distinct elements that should be used in conjunction for truly safe practice.

1. Encryption

This is the electronic equivalent of putting a message in an envelope (see Figure 2.1.1). It protects confidentiality and confirms for the recipient that the message has arrived in its original state without having been seen by an unauthorised person. Good encryption software ensures that information is only decrypted as and when needed, and then makes provision for the safe deletion of electronic messages. This would have the same effect that a shredding machine has on paper that needs to be destroyed.

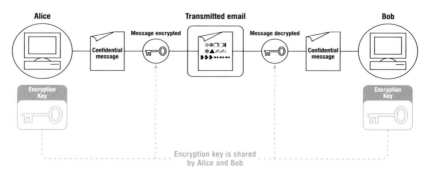

Figure 2.1.1 Message encryption

2. Digital signature

This is the electronic equivalent of signing and sealing a letter by hand (see Figure 2.1.2). It maintains the integrity, authenticity and non-repudiation aspects of an email in much the same way as a personal hand-written signature is proof of authorship of a letter. Digital signatures are an even greater guarantee of authenticity than their hand-written counterparts as they cannot be forged. An email that has been digitally signed ensures that the message cannot be repudiated or considered invalid (ie denied by the sender).

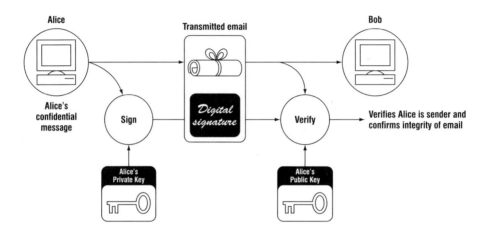

Figure 2.1.2 Digital signature

Cryptographic techniques and digital signatures, though widely available for both private and business use and simple in concept, can nevertheless be technically difficult solutions to understand for someone with poor IT knowledge. This should not, however, deter users from further investigation; for with a little effort the solution will come to light. Misinformation or inadequate education of IT security (both in terms of possible solutions and knowledge of what constitutes the biggest threats to that security) go some way towards explaining the apparent reluctance to embrace the available technology.

Perceived barriers to securing email

Email encryption and virus detection software

One of the biggest perceived problems regarding IT security faced by business users is the widely held belief that encrypted email messages would bypass anti-virus and content-checking server-based software. This is exacerbated by the fact that the equally potent threats posed by hackers and viruses now frequently converge, the Code Red Worm (2001) being a good example of this. As such, the use of cryptographic tools is not as common as it should be.[6] Companies frequently use as explanation for their failure to make adequate security provisions for email the fact that cryptographic technology has not been implemented because of the need to scan incoming messages for viruses and inappropriate content.

Because of this confusion, many businesses have failed to protect their electronically transmitted information instead of aiming to find appropriate solutions. The simple fact that has been largely overlooked by the IT departments of most organisations is that anti-virus software and encryption techniques are actually compatible, and if this crucial misunderstanding were to be rectified, email users could enjoy far greater security and peace of mind. There is no reason why email users should be under the impression that serious vulnerability is something they must accept if they want to transmit information over the Internet. Anti-virus software is only rendered ineffective by encryption software when it is installed on a network server. When, on the other hand, the installation is made at desktop level, the two sets of software are fully complementary, which in conjunction with the firewall gives the user a sound level of security.

There is a very wide range of anti-virus products available on the market, many of which are fully compatible with cryptographic techniques and which can be installed locally. In cases where the anti-virus software cannot be installed locally, the email rules inherent in encryption software are so flexible that users are able to determine which messages are encrypted and which are not.

By combining the use of solid encryption techniques and careful rule-setting with modern, desktop-based, anti-virus software, comprehensive and effective control of email security would lie entirely, and independently, with the user.

Plugging the hole

Rather than being baffled by the technology, businesses need to be clear about their security needs and to choose modern encryption software with good functionality that they understand completely.

Businesses need to recognise that unprotected email is a risk. It is a vulnerability that cannot be fixed by a firewall installation or by anti-virus implementation. A security policy that does not address the open nature of emails is falling short of its purpose. Email usage is too prolific not to assign an appropriate level of protection to it. Its use will not diminish – it is here to stay – and legislation will dictate that businesses must apply sound security measures. Until businesses start to follow these recommendations for the protection of their intellectual property and confidential communications – which are both extremely vulnerable for as long as unsecured emails are committed to cyberspace – no amount of spending on firewalls or anti-virus software will constitute adequate protection for their IT systems.

---

[6] According to a DTI report published earlier this year, only 35 per cent of UK businesses that provide employees with Internet email (48 per cent of large businesses) have the ability to encrypt emails passing over the Internet, and only 29 per cent (36 per cent of large businesses) can digitally sign Internet email.

For further information on email security contact: Charlotte Cowell, Indicii Salus, Indiccii Salus House, 2 Beffborough Gardens, London SW1V 2JE. Tel: +44 (0)20 7592 3022; Fax: +44 (0)20 7836 0567; Email: ccowell@indiciisalus.com; Website: www.indiciisalus.com

Web security

Internet software was generally designed with security as an afterthought. Unfortunately the consequences can be disastrous, warns Sam Green of Zeus Technology.

History

Security holes in business-critical software are a significant threat to organisations. However, vulnerabilities in Internet-related software can be disastrous. In a recent survey, respondents said that 70 per cent of their security attacks occurred through their Internet connection.

Ironically, Internet software was generally designed with security as an afterthought. Networks were largely considered to be either private and therefore physically secure, or public and therefore inherently open. With the enormous growth in the Internet as a medium for business, this assumption is extremely dated; and coupled with a limited understanding of the requirements for truly securing an online offering, we are currently paying the price for a history of non-secure software design.

In some areas this mindset still has not changed. For example, wireless local area networks (LANs) became popular and cost-effective in 2001, and with their rise in popularity it was only a matter of time before hacking tools for this medium were created. On 12 April 2001 'WEPcrack' was released. WEP is the encryption method used to protect data sent across a wireless link, and through the use of WEPcrack an attacker can quickly compromise security on a network. WEP is a modern design, but it highlights the fact that software designers still see security as an afterthought.

The amount of private information transmitted across the Internet increases daily. It is now an integral part of most people's lives, ranging from buying books at Amazon on a credit card through to making money transfers and payments via an online bank. For businesses it is even more ingrained; organisations typically use the Internet to sell goods and services and to perform stock control via trusted links to supply chain partners.

Potentially there are numerous reasons for the growth in security attacks; but one trend that is undeniable is the growth in the number and sophistication of hacking tools. Historically attackers required detailed understanding of the systems that they were attempting to compromise, and performing an attack could be a time-consuming operation. The sophistication of tools such as NMAP, BackOrifice and other similar tools has brought about a rise in the number of novice attackers (sometimes referred to as 'script kiddies'). These attackers have very little understanding of system security, attack methods and avoiding detection; however, with modern hacking tools this is largely irrelevant.

Statistics show that over 300,000 hosts were infected by Internet worms like 'Code Red' and 'Nimda' during the past two years. The cost of Code Red is estimated to be approximately US$2 billion, making it the second costliest outbreak ever (*Information Security*, September 2001). These two worms are not the only ones; in fact there is a long history of similar events.

The first recorded Internet worm was released in 1988. It used a buffer overflow in the finger service on UNIX systems. Written by a student, this worm severely affected 6,000 systems and the entire Internet came to a near standstill.

For many years, writing worms and viruses was a secret activity until Aleph One wrote an article called 'Smashing the Stack for Fun and Profit', which was published in *Phrack* magazine. His paper described in great detail how to exploit buffer overflow problems on a UNIX system. Many people started writing their own viruses and worms to attack other systems, especially open source software, because the source code was available and problems could be found by reading the code. In 1997 and 1998, almost weekly updates of widely used software like the mail server Sendmail were common.

In 1999 the list of known exploits had continued to grow, but for the first time there were exploits aimed against Microsoft products. Microsoft was shielded from these problems because the operating system and all its applications were written in a completely different style to applications for UNIX; and, at the time, Microsoft was largely focused on desktop operating systems or basic workgroup functionality rather than being a credible Internet server operating system – which had traditionally been UNIX hackers' operating system of choice.

There also was no source code available to read to find security vulnerabilities. Dildog's paper on how to exploit Microsoft applications opened the door to many hackers. Initially it might have been harder to find weaknesses in Microsoft applications, but once they were found it was possible to use almost any functionality that the Windows operating system provided in order to spread the virus or worm. Because the process and security model in Microsoft's operating systems was very easy to break into and exploit – coupled with the explosion in PC users – it quickly became very popular to write viruses and other tools to exploit all these weaknesses. Tools like Back Orifice and NetBus became very popular and allowed a large number of amateur hackers to create havoc on the general PC-owning population.

The threat

Today security is a bigger problem than ever before. PCs are everywhere; every organisation has some form of Internet access, and home users have permanent connections through broadband, but user education is still relatively limited.

This is partly due to the multitude of attack methods and the frequency of attacks. Users are required to use and maintain anti-virus programs to protect against viruses transmitted over networks, via email, via dangerous ActiveX components and through a host of other transport methods. With the growth in Internet use, a large number of organisations have adopted Microsoft's IIS web server; and with large-scale adoption come large-scale attacks. Increasingly, IIS web servers are being attacked by worms that exploit their security weaknesses. Worms are programs that spread without any human intervention. Once a worm is released onto the Internet it will automatically try to find other vulnerable hosts and infect them.

The most dangerous forms of Internet worm are those that attack web servers. Unlike the average Internet connection, these systems have network connections with large amounts of bandwidth. After an infection, a worm can use the bandwidth to spread itself to other web servers. Equally, the organisation operating the web server may base a large percentage of its revenue on traffic from its website, and the site outage could cause a large-scale financial impact – not to mention the impact on customer confidence. All worms follow the same general scheme outlined below.

Infection

Infection involves the worm sending a malicious request to a web server, trying to exploit a known security vulnerability. If the web server is vulnerable, the worm infects the machine, executes its payload and then continues to spread to other machines.

Some web servers, such as Microsoft IIS, run in privileged kernel space because it can result in large performance improvements. Unfortunately, together with the increased performance comes a very serious security risk.

A web server that does not run in kernel space, such as Zeus, restricts the impact that an attacker could have because the web server is generally operating under the control of a non-privileged user. Therefore, if an attacker is successful in compromising a web server that runs in user space, the attacker must then try to break into an administrative or other privileged account before any serious damage can be done.

Any security exploit used against a web server that operates in kernel space (such as Microsoft IIS) is extremely dangerous. The worm does not need to break any security barriers to get access to the core of the operating system; the compromised web server immediately allows it access to the highest user/kernel privilege. The many complex layers of APIs and extended functionality within IIS create a number of possible weak points to exploit.

Traditionally, one of the major strengths of the UNIX operating system has been the integrity of the kernel; however, even organisations in the UNIX market have started to create kernel-based web servers to try and gain a performance edge over user space applications.

Install a spreading mechanism

Once a Microsoft IIS server has been infected with a worm, the worm's code can make use of software available on the system and, furthermore, even download additional software from other systems. During this phase the worm installs itself on the machine and starts to work independently.

Optional: Install or modify other services

Some worms install backdoor services to give hackers access to machines. They are then able to control the system remotely and use it for future exploits, such as distributed denial of service attacks. 'Code Red', for example, checks if the web server is running with the English (US) language pack installed and then defaces the website with a banner saying 'Hacked by the Chinese'. This is a relatively obvious payload and one that is likely to be detected relatively quickly. A potential payload could be far more sinister and could surreptitiously transmit important data, such as credit-card details, to a remote machine.

Search for new systems

In order to be able to infect other systems every worm needs some form of reproduction mechanism. It needs to find new servers to which it can spread by investigating the addresses of potential targets. Due to the very unbalanced nature of 1Pv4 address space it would make very little sense to work through the entire Internet in a step-by-step process. Worm developers have been creative when it comes to engineering an efficient algorithm to find as many likely targets as possible. Currently, the most efficient mechanism is to write a program that is able to behave differently on every infected host; ideally every infected host would have completely different lists of hosts it tries to attack. Most search algorithms are based on the infected host's IP address and network. Code Red focused on attacking servers on the same subnet, which created large amounts of traffic across backbone networks. In a number of cases this surge in traffic created denial of service attacks. Another interesting approach would be to use external resources that gather details of web servers such as MediaMetrix or Netcraft to find as many web servers as possible – this was suggested by Nicholas Weaver in a recent paper on Internet worm propagation.

Optional: Attack other systems

Many worms have built-in attack routines. For example, Code Red tried to perform a distributed denial of service attack on an IP address belonging to the White House website (www.whitehouse.gov). The target server was moved to a different location after the worm was dissected by forensic security analysts, with the result that the attack failed. However, the worm could easily be rewritten to dynamically gather attack data from a number of sources that would overcome this limitation. Far more dangerous are worms that install a distributed denial of service slave that goes instantly to 'sleep' and does not affect other local services on the machine. These slaves can then be activated by remote controllers, thereby causing large floods of attacks within a few seconds.

Business implications

The web is a vital component of an organisation's infrastructure. Companies cannot afford downtime, public defacement or leakage of confidential customer and company information. The financial implications can be enormous and the impact on customer confidence can be catastrophic.

The solutions

As with the security for your business premises, an intruder will always look for the easiest way in; if you can make it sufficiently secure then they will go elsewhere. Internet security is not a matter of installing one system, but of looking at all the components in your systems to see if they offer any holes. Installing systems that are secure in the first place obviously means less work than installing insecure ones and then trying to secure them.

Over the past 24 months there have been so many high-profile attacks on Microsoft IIS servers that Gartner has advised organisations that take their web infrastructure seriously to look at migrating away from IIS. More recently, worms have been released to attack Apache servers running under UNIX.

If your business relies on its website, then you should talk to an organisation like Zeus Technology who specialise in advising organisations about their Internet infrastructure, including issues of security. Don't wait to install the locks until after you've been burgled!

Zeus Technology is the world's expert on hosting automation and web infrastructure solutions. Zeus provides software that leads the industry in performance, scalability, reliability and security, combined with support and consultancy services that provide best-of-breed solutions for business-critical Internet deployments for leading web-hosting, content providing and e-commerce companies.

Zeus has created a highly scalable and robust line of software products including the multi-award winning Zeus Web Server, Zeus Load Balancer and Zeus Mass Hosting Application. Zeus boasts an impressive customer and strategic partner base, which includes world-class companies such as eBay, HP, IBM, AMD, Sun Microsystems, SGI, Sprint, Cable & Wireless, Telefonica, Telewest, NEC Biglobe, THUS/Demon and Qualcomm, which has enabled the company to achieve consistent growth since its formation in 1995.

For further information contact: Sam Green, Zeus Technology, Tel: +44 (0)1223 525 000; Email: sgreen@zeus.com; Website:http://www.zeus.com

Network vulnerabilities

Network technology is being turned inside out from a security perspective, writes Peter Crowcombe, EMEA Marketing Manager of NetScreen Technologies, Inc. Extranets and wireless networks make organisations inherently more vulnerable to attack.

Basic security tenets have changed very little over the past decade. Protecting the confidentiality of corporate information, preventing unauthorised access and defending against malicious or fraudulent attacks from external sources: these continue to be the major concerns of IT professionals today. To defend against such threats, IT managers have traditionally deployed security solutions at the periphery of their network.

Now, however, networks are being turned inside out from a security perspective. For example, more and more organisations are turning to wireless local area networks (WLANs) to connect to the public Internet; extranets are becoming an increasingly popular way of linking to and communicating with partners, customers, consultants and suppliers. Such developments make an enterprise's network inherently more vulnerable to attack and more readily breached. The 'bad guys' are becoming smarter too, in terms of capitalising on these vulnerabilities. Worms, trojan horse attacks and viruses that lie dormant and then launch themselves from within the network are commonplace nowadays. Intrusions from hackers may sabotage or gain control of network servers, data files and other resources such as databases.

Additionally, the Internet exposes organisations to security risks such as denial of service attacks that can cripple e-business applications and jeopardise both revenue streams and customer goodwill. Disgruntled and dishonest employees are also becoming more 'computer savvy', capable of perpetrating mischievous and illegal acts in order to damage corporate data on the network. In just one example from many thousands of incidents, a clerk in a broker's firm altered computer records, illegally changing the ownership and price of 1,700 shares.

People working from home – telecommuters – and employees who are connecting to the network whilst travelling – road warriors – can also open up 'holes' in a network's boundary that can be easily exploited. Even well-meaning, but careless or ill-informed, employees surfing the public Internet can compromise the entire organisation's data integrity. In short, the periphery of the network is no longer the only place to secure it; the so-called 'trusted' part of the network – that is, the part that lies behind the boundary with the outside world – has disappeared.

To compound the threat posed by these developments, networks are also operating at much higher speeds. Of course, increased speed is a great advantage when legitimate data is traversing the network, but it also means that illegitimate traffic can traverse and attack the network with equal speed. So the security solution must be smarter and more pervasive within the network, be able to match the speed of the network infrastructure, and be easily adapted to the security requirements of emerging technologies.

Better ways to resolve network vulnerabilities

The fundamental key to an effective security solution is a properly deployed network security device that increases security without jeopardising performance. To meet the many and varied threats already outlined, multi-functionality within a single platform can ease network design and maximise effectiveness. Solid inter-operability with other security products, such as user authentication and anti-virus applications, will also prove invaluable.

Software security solutions – those that perform firewall and Virtual Private Network (VPN) functions via a processor on a dedicated, but standard PC, or dedicated processor hardware platform – have been the traditional 'legacy' solution. However, in this new generation of varied and increasing security threats, they are widely regarded as too slow. This causes two problems: first, they cannot keep pace should an attack on the network occur; and second, they have to slow down legitimate data in order to check it, causing a bottleneck or chokepoint. This largely negates any investment made in a high-speed network infrastructure and creates a great deal of frustration on the part of users.

A security solution running on a PC either has to rely upon the third-party operating system, or have the operating system 'hardened'. The former makes the whole solution extremely vulnerable, as the workings of most standard PC operating systems are very well known to the hacker community worldwide and are, therefore, easy to breach. The latter approach makes it more difficult to breach a system, but it only slightly increases protection and also creates extra work and expense each time a new security device is brought online into the network. Another problem with the software approach to security is that the software and the processor together mean two points of potential failure – or twice the risk of something going wrong and leaving the network unprotected. From a management point of view, the software approach to security can be complex – individual users of the software that has been brought online have to be licensed and this must be renewed annually. Of course, this means renewals are staggered randomly throughout the year, creating a complex and laborious task in maintaining them all.

A new generation of security devices based upon Application-Specific Integrated Circuit (ASIC) technology – in other words, microchips that are programmed to perform security functions such as firewalling and VPN encryption – has emerged to address the vulnerabilities present in the legacy approach. ASICs can be built into dedicated security platforms with multiple functions. ASIC-based solutions can operate at high speeds, easily keeping pace with the surrounding infrastructure and performing various security-related tasks simultaneously. As they function from within a dedicated, 'closed' platform, ASIC-based solutions have a proprietary, or tailor-made operating system that is not common knowledge in the outside world and therefore less vulnerable than prior designs on standard PC/server platforms. Another advantage of the hardware approach is that the correct hardware device is deployed to fit the capacity of users from the outset, so individual licences are not required.

Protecting the 'trusted' network

Once a network security solution that addresses the fundamentals of performance and reliability is identified, it then has to be evaluated for its ability to provide pervasive internal protection. In essence, identifying a security solution that provides the ability to segment a network and establish security zones is critical to protecting against emerging internal threats.

Establishing security zones enables protection of distinct network segments (eg those servers handling marketing, sales, finance and human resources). For instance, an employee in the marketing department who is curious about other people's salaries will not be able to access human resources data; they will be denied access from within the network, just as a snooper would be externally. Segmenting the network into distinct security zones also limits the potential damage by an external hacker who has been successful in breaching the boundary of the network. If network servers are kept separate from one another (from a security perspective), any illegal incursion can be contained within just one zone. Similarly, VPN tunnels can be directed into a specific security zone, so that any network links with external parties can be terminated and secured in the appropriate zone, avoiding unnecessary risk for other zones' data and servers.

A 'virtual' approach to establishing security zones is required to efficiently enable segmentation. Selecting security devices with virtual system capabilities can reduce the overall number of devices in a network and thereby streamline security management, reducing the total cost of ownership. With certain virtual system-enabled devices, different policies can be applied to different zones, depending on each department's need for access to sensitive information, the type and number of employees, etc.

So, in conclusion, although basic network issues have remained largely the same, new business practices and emerging technologies are making protection against these threats more challenging than ever before. Changing levels of trust, constantly evolving external threats, and computer-literate employees with potential grudges, are collectively putting the enterprise on edge. The careful selection, deployment and management of best-in-breed network security technology that helps reduce costs without sacrificing performance can provide a realistic and effective answer to the challenge.

Key security vocabulary explained

VPNs: virtual private networks create a secure tunnel between two points, typically a corporate network central office and a remote branch office. The tunnel passes encrypted (scrambled) data over the public Internet, then decrypts it at the destination point. This protects data from hackers on its path over the Internet, and renders the data unreadable during its journey.

Denial of service: This is a hacker-based attack on a web server that prevents customers/visitors from gaining access to an organisation's website. Usually launched by a worm virus (eg Code Red, Code Blue) that can replicate from computer to computer. There are also 'distributed denial of service' attacks, which simultaneously attack several servers at once.

Firewall: This is a system that provides both network access control and attack containment features to prevent and block unauthorised traffic entering the corporate network. A firewall checks each passing packet of data in respect of its starting point, destination, content, size etc.

Intrusion prevention: This detects network, application and hybrid attacks and provides alarms to network operators. It also has the ability to 'drop' the attack from the network to stop it from reaching its target.

Trojan Horse: This is an attack that is hidden within a seemingly legitimate attachment to an email received across the Internet. Once inside a PC it infects memory, processor and applications, then spreads to other network resources. In some cases it will establish contact with the hacker, enabling tunnels or embedded controls to infiltrate the corporate network.

Backdoor or U-turn attacks: These are methods of network attack aimed at small branch offices that have Internet access both locally and via the corporate VPN. Illegal entry is gained via the local link and, once behind the remote site's VPN, the hacker can strike the corporate network via the VPN.

WLANs: Wireless local area networks are created using a broadcast medium. Wireless hackers are particularly dangerous as they can gain access to the network by broadcast proximity to the network (for example, in a car or on foot near the building where the WLAN is in operation).

Virus: A computer virus attacks by 'piggy-backing' on top of another program in order to be executed. Once it is running, it is then able to infect other programs or data files.

NetScreen Technologies Inc is a leading developer of integrated network security solutions that offer the security, performance and total cost of ownership required by enterprises and carriers. NetScreen's innovative solutions provide key security technologies, such as virtual private networks, denial of service protection, and firewall and intrusion prevention, in a line of easy-to-manage security appliances and systems. NetScreen is publicly traded on the NASDAQ market under the symbol NSCN.

For further information contact: Company Headquarters at 350 Oakmead Parkway, Sunnyvale, CA 94085, USA. Regional headquarters for Asia-Pacific and Europe are located in Hong Kong and Guildford, UK, respectively. More information on NetScreen's products in Europe can be found at www.netscreen.com or by calling 08700 75 00 00.

Remote working

Remote working can open up a company to new threats from hackers unless the right precautionary measures are put in place, writes Paul Drew from Tekdata.

In today's Internet-driven world the use of the teleworker is becoming more common. This is good for both workers and businesses as it reduces overheads and travelling time, increases productivity through flexible working and also allows companies to recruit the quality of staff they need even though they may not live near the companies' offices.

Over 80 per cent of companies now have staff who work from home on a regular or occasional basis, according to the latest research. A survey carried out by SonicWALL Inc shows that 83 per cent of companies now allow teleworking, with 43 per cent having staff who access the company's network from home, usually via the Internet.

Big businesses are more likely to encourage the practice than their smaller cousins. Home working is now prevalent in 98 per cent of large companies (with £20 million or more turnover) compared with 91 per cent of small-to-medium sized enterprises (with £5–20 million turnover) and 79 per cent of small businesses (with £1–5 million turnover).

Once the main method of connecting the remote worker to the corporate system was through point-to-point dial-up connections; but now, with technological advances and increasing Internet-driven business activities, remote workers can easily connect from anywhere in the world. Using VPNs (Virtual Private Networks) teleworkers are connecting to corporate networks and accessing day-to-day business-critical systems and information.

This process has led to many domestic networks being created within remote workers' homes, and increasingly these networks or laptops are being used by the whole family. Activities such as file swapping, instant messaging, online gaming and video conferencing can inadvertently open up back-door holes for hackers to hijack corporate VPNs.

Directors, under new data protection laws, are now legally responsible for information held on corporate networks concerning their employees and customers. Various systems can create a 'trusted zone' of network security between the corporate office and the telecommuter, protecting your corporate network against malicious intrusions that occur when work computers share broadband Internet access with multiple-networked family computers. This trusted zone ensures that harmful intrusion cannot traverse the home network to the corporate network, and that in-home users cannot access the corporate network.

Tekdata is a specialist distributor of upgrade, replacement and new-technology products whose focus is the supply of general and storage peripherals, Internet access and security, biometrics VoIP and electronic component packaging products.

For further information contact: Tekdata (Network Solutions and Distribution), Westport House, Federation Road, Burslem, Stoke on Trent, Staffordshire ST6 4HY. Tel: +44 (0)1782 254777; Fax: +44 (0)1782 834784; Email: teksales@tekdata.co.uk

Protecting online privacy

It pays to observe data privacy, says Simon Stokes at Tarlo Lyons Solicitors, not just to avoid legal liability, but to enhance the value of the data itself.

In recent years laws protecting the privacy of individuals when personal data about them is stored or processed have proliferated internationally. These laws deal with data privacy and (as it is called in Europe) data protection. All UK e-commerce businesses must comply with data protection law. This is not just to avoid legal liability; by paying careful attention to compliance issues the value of a company's data can be significantly enhanced. For example, compliance may allow you to conduct direct marketing or to sell data to a third party (if, for instance, your business is sold).

Under the Data Protection Act 1998 ('Act') the general rule is that anyone using personal data (which could be as simple as a name and address or even an email address) must notify their processing of the data to the UK's Information Commissioner. Failure to do so is a criminal offence. The Information Commissioner can also take legal action where there are other breaches of data protection law. In particular the eight data protection principles in the Act must be complied with, namely:

1. Personal data shall be processed fairly and lawfully.
2. Personal data shall only be obtained for one or more specified and lawful purpose.
3. Personal data shall be adequate, relevant and not excessive in relation to the purpose or purposes for which they are processed.
4. Personal data shall be accurate and, where necessary, kept up to date.

5. Personal data processed for any purpose or purposes shall not be kept for longer than is necessary.
6. Personal data shall be processed in accordance with the rights of data subjects.
7. Appropriate technical and organisational measures shall be taken against unauthorised or unlawful processing of personal data and against accidental loss or destruction of, or damage to, personal data.
8. Personal data shall not be transferred to a country or territory outside the European Economic Area unless that country or territory ensures an adequate level of protection for the rights and freedoms of data subjects in relation to the processing of personal data.

Persons who suffer harm as a result of unlawful processing or other breaches of the Act are also entitled to claim damages against the business concerned. There are also special rules for 'sensitive personal data' – ethnicity, health records, membership of a trade union, etc.

The need for a privacy statement

Where a business collects personal data – for example, contact details and other data such as customer preferences – via a web page or email, the business must ensure that the personal data is fairly and lawfully processed. It must also be obtained only for one or more specified and lawful purposes and must not be processed in a manner incompatible with these purposes. In practice this includes making sure that you have an online privacy statement in the proper form, which is brought to the attention of those submitting personal data. The privacy statement must clearly set out the purposes for which the data is collected and processed. Where the data will be used for direct marketing purposes current practice is to include an 'opt out' box, giving the person the right not to have their data used for this purpose. The privacy statement can also help you to comply with other areas of the Act, for example if the data is to be transferred (exported) outside Europe for processing.

Data exports

The current law (under the eighth data protection principle) is that personal data can only be exported outside Europe if the country to which the data is exported has an adequate level of protection. The United States is not considered to have this, for example. Where the importing country does not have this level of protection, it may be possible to resolve the situation by having the data exporting and data importing parties enter into a 'model form contract' approved by the EU. Or the importing country concerned may have its own voluntary regime, such as the US 'safe harbor' regime. Where the prior consent to the transfer of the data subjects (that is, the persons about whom personal data is held and processed) is obtained, then there is no need to worry about 'model clauses' etc; the transfer will be lawful. Where possible, this is the best course of action. A carefully drafted online privacy statement can help too.

Security

The seventh data protection principle requires that 'appropriate technical and organisational measures shall be taken against unauthorised or unlawful processing of personal data and against accidental loss or destruction of, or damage to, personal data'. In other words, the data must be kept secure. This is particularly important when the data may be available online and where there is a risk that it may become available to others. To comply with this principle it is typical to conduct a risk assessment of current data security measures. Also, any third-party data processors (for example, persons you have outsourced to) must be under a written contractual obligation to ensure that personal data are kept secure.

Spamming and direct marketing

The current law

The current law in this area is complex – involving the Data Protection Act 1998 and the Telecommunications (Data Protection and Privacy) Regulations 1999 (as amended). It requires that the making of automated calls or sending automated faxes by way of direct marketing must have the prior consent of the recipient (ie an 'opt in'). Where unsolicited non-automated calls or faxes are sent or made then the relevant 'opt out' register, kept by the Director General of Telecommunications, must be consulted in advance. If the recipient of a fax is an individual subscriber rather than a company, then a prior 'opt in' must always be obtained. Customer preferences communicated to the sender or caller must also be respected.

For direct marketing sent by email or 'snail mail' (post/courier), the recipient has the right to opt out. Of course, the person processing the data for direct marketing purposes must be compliant with data protection law generally as well – for example, their privacy statement should deal with direct marketing.

The new law

The 2002 Directive on Privacy and Electronic Communications ('Directive'), which must be implemented into UK law before 31 October 2003, sets out a new regime regulating unsolicited communications for direct marketing sent by:

■ automatic calling machines (use of automated calling systems without human intervention);
■ fax;
■ electronic mail (this includes SMS text messages).

These are only allowed where subscribers have given their prior consent – ie 'opt in' applies. However, where there is an existing customer relationship, and electronic contact details are obtained in the context of a *sale* of a product or service, then you are allowed to use email to market to customers in the future for your own *similar* products or services. But you must give customers the right to opt out when their email details are collected initially and then each time you send a subsequent direct marketing email.

For other unsolicited electronic communications for direct marketing (eg by telephone or mobile phone) the UK will be able to choose whether there is an 'opt in' or 'opt out' regime.

Also any direct marketing electronic mail must not disguise or conceal the identity of the sender and must have a valid address for the receipt of any 'opt out'. This is in addition to the requirements of the Electronic Commerce Regulations 2002, which also deal with the need to identify unsolicited 'commercial communications' as such, and with other online information requirements.

Cookies, web crawlers, spiders, web bugs

These technologies potentially allow third parties access to the contents of your computer. A 'cookie' is a small text file that is stored on the hard drive of your computer when you visit a website. Their purpose is to allow repeat visits (eg by a subscriber to the site) and they can also be used to gather information about you.

Web bugs, spyware and other similar devices can be used to gain access to information on your computer, to store hidden information and to trace your activities. They are used typically for clandestine purposes.

The new Directive sees 'cookies' as a legitimate and useful tool. However, web bugs and similar devices are seen as a serious threat to privacy, and they must only be used for legitimate purposes with the knowledge of the users concerned. The use of 'cookies' is permitted provided that:

■ the user is given clear and comprehensive information about the use to be made of the information gathered by the cookie – this must be made as 'user friendly' as possible; and
■ the user has the opportunity to refuse the cookie. However, access to a website can be made conditional on the user's well-informed acceptance of a cookie.

Conclusion

Dealing with online privacy issues is just part of dealing with data protection compliance more generally. Areas typically included in any compliance programme are:

■ existence and role of a compliance officer and management involvement;
■ internal staff policies and awareness of procedures and sanctions for non-compliance;
■ website privacy statements and processes of collecting personal data; duration of data retention;
■ staff monitoring;
■ handling of requests by data subjects to access their personal data;
■ security standards applied (both technical and operational).

Looking more specifically at online privacy issues, privacy statements are essential when addresses or personal data are collected. Where email/telephone numbers are to be used for direct marketing (eg by email or SMS) then best practice will be to obtain prior 'explicit' consent, for example by a tick in an 'I consent' box on a web form. Information must also be put in place dealing with cookies, and users must be able to refuse them.

Where personal data will be transferred outside the EU for processing, it is essential that either consent is obtained or other compliance options are investigated.

Tarlo Lyons is a leading London law firm focused on delivering commercial solutions for technology-driven business. It has one of the largest teams of dedicated technology lawyers in England, and believes in leveraging the expertise and talent it has assembled to provide real benefits for its clients. It believes that success comes from contributing to its client's objectives, and its ability to understand and work with technology is central to this.

For further information contact: Tarlo Lyons, Watchmaker Court, 33 St John's Lane, London EC1M 4DB. Tel: +44 (0)20 7405 2000; Fax: +44 (0)20 7814 9421; Email: Simon.Stokes@tarlolyons.com; Website: www.tarlolyons.com

Online payments

Making online payments secure is not just about fighting fraud – it also makes good business sense, says APACS's Head of Security Colin Whittaker.

The defeat of fraud, as the banking sector migrates to conducting more and more payments online, is of critical concern to the industry and the consumer. Colin Whittaker is confident that the industry is up to this challenge: no bank's payments systems have been cracked. 'I don't believe anyone has ever broken into a payment system. I am not being glib by saying that just honest. Security is the primary asset in the banking industry.'

APACS has a major programme to keep abreast of potential new risks. It does, however, face the problem that the technological environment is always changing, with the goalposts continually being moved: 'We are always having to appraise what new threats are out there and what assets need to be protected.' Whilst it is easy to see how threats change over time, it is also important to recognise that the types of assets that need to be protected can change over time as well. For instance customers' details and accounts have become a critical asset for the industry to protect with the implementation of the Data Protection Act 1988.

Some of the risks the industry itself can't do anything about. Instead, they have to rely on business to act in an appropriate manner: 'Some SMEs deal with their payments in the same way as consumers – with credit cards and debit cards – and so face the same obligations and risks as consumers do with their cards. As these businesses increase in complexity and size they face new challenges, especially from staff. They start becoming vulnerable to insider risks.'

Businesses use a range of payment systems and vehicles provided by the banking sector. These are being enhanced to action payments between businesses and between businesses and consumers in an online environment. Commercial online banking is similar to retail banking, only more sophisticated and with more services and capabilities. Colin says:

'Businesses are being delivered a product that has security at the heart of it, but we must recognise that they are potentially being operated in an insecure environment. Businesses must be prepared to secure their own IT environment with as much attention as a consumer secures their own debit and credit cards in their wallet.'

There is a lot of guidance on internal controls such as the international security standard BS 7799 (www.ukonlineforbusiness.gov.uk/inforsec). This helps identify risks for business – whether they are physical or procedural. There is a whole raft of technological strategies that businesses can use to secure their electronic environment such as firewalls and unique user passwords, which are discussed elsewhere in this book. Credit cards such as Visa and Mastercard have also produced guidelines on, for instance, how to store customer information. The DTI is also developing a website to provide guidance to SMEs through the main UK Online for Business website: www.ukonlineforbusiness.gov.uk. APACS is supporting the development of this website.

Colin says that the key for businesses (particularly those at the smaller end of the SME scale) is to weigh up the risks of a security breach compared to the assets that may be compromised. How business manages and implements security as it applies to their online payment systems is critical. This boils down to balancing personnel measures, such as how employees are recruited and trained; procedural measures, such as the management of employee accounts, passwords, and how often systems are reviewed and audited; and technical measures such as patch updates and antivirus products to achieve cost-effective security.

'Companies have to delve into the costs and benefits and make their own judgement call. They have to think about the broader costs and benefits vis-à-vis the fraud cost. It is too simplistic to say that security measure 'A' counters fraud 'X'. Many security measures may also act to streamline, simplify and cut overheads.' He says that security can enhance the business, and this should also be taken into account when making decisions about security. For instance, with secure online banking a company can look at its cashflow on a daily basis and can see when it is more prudent to invest or when it is a good time to make particular payments. There is also the time saved. So security should be part of broader business decisions.

On the horizon Colin sees the NewBACS programme, which is upgrading and modernising the direct debiting and standing order processing payment systems, having wider applicability than the current system, which will make it more useful for smaller companies and SMEs: 'As the technology and security enhances there will be a lot more benefits to SMEs.'

The growth of plastic card payments, once they have been made more secure, will lead to savings for smaller SMEs who might normally use cheques for payments. Colin says: 'The SME sector is one with a surprisingly high reliance on cheques. One of the reasons often given is the need for accountability, with many companies requiring two people to sign a cheque to make it valid. However, in order for SMEs to achieve savings from using plastic payment cards they will need to determine what levels of internal accountability and trust their businesses need.' He says the industry is already rolling out plastic payment cards that contain smartcards that will enhance their security for payments and other banking applications: 'The industry is examining low-cost hand-held devices that can use these cards to generate one-time-only passwords, or offer a challenge and response mechanism that could be used in a range of financial applications. These devices are as small as the credit card itself.'

But it is not all rosy in the field of online payments and banks; businesses and consumers must continue to be vigilant, because as soon as technology is available to improve security, ironically, people try to break these new secure systems: 'Attackers have become a lot smarter and we have to stay one step ahead of them. The technology they are using has become more capable and powerful. At the same time the level of complexity and sophistication of systems in day-to-day use by consumers and businesses continues to increase, unfortunately, because of this complexity, with hidden and unknown vulnerabilities that may only be exposed at some time in the future.'

APACS is the UK trade association of banks and building societies that exchange payments on behalf of their customers. It also has responsibility for the co-operative aspects of money transmission and other payments-related developments.

For further information contact: Association for Payment Clearing Services, Mercury House, Triton Court, 14 Finsbury Square, London EC2A 1LQ. Tel: +44 (0)20 7711 6200; Fax: +44 (0)20 7256 5527.

Case study: Wellbeing.com takes a dose of the ClearCommerce medicine

When Boots Company plc and Granada plc unveiled www.wellbeing.com, the organisations expected the website to draw much attention from customers wanting to access information and purchase goods. However, they also realised that it would attract fraudsters interested in acquiring luxury items such as CDs, perfumes and fitness equipment. As a result, a highly scalable and resilient website with strong fraud protection was needed. They turned to ClearCommerce to support this requirement. Following an £18 million investment, wellbeing.com was launched to offer an 'e-store' featuring around 10,000 items.

A painful operation

Boots already had some experience of online retailing having originally launched a transactional website at www.boots.co.uk. This version included a basic PC BACS link to its acquiring bank, Barclays Merchant Services (BMS) and Natwest. But once orders were received, the transactions were manually re-keyed into the point-of-sale system, making customer service a slow and cumbersome task.

Just what the doctor ordered

Kevin Figgitt, third-party operations manager at wellbeing.com, said: 'In the highly competitive world of e-tailing, success is ensured through the provision of a customer-friendly and fraud free shopping experience.'

Internet fraud doesn't just affect customer loyalty. Because credit card purchases over the Internet are classified as card-not-present transactions, wellbeing.com is 100 per cent liable for losses, even when the bank has authorised the transaction. For wellbeing.com, the cost of Internet fraud includes direct costs, such as the costs of goods sold, bank charge-back fees and higher discount rates. There are also indirect costs, such as the cost of tracking and handling fraudulent transactions.

The remedy

To combat these problems wellbeing.com turned to ClearCommerce for its Enterprise Merchant Engine, a real-time transaction processing software solution.

Wellbeing.com wanted a platform that could seamlessly send transactions to BMS. ClearCommerce's Enterprise Merchant Engine was the obvious solution as the system is accredited by BMS, which meant that time did not have to be wasted in writing software codes to enable transactions.

Once the customer clicks the 'buy' button, the ClearCommerce transaction management software enables a real-time connection between the merchant's store-front and the credit/debit card processors to authorise card transactions. This procedure minimises the problems caused later in the fulfilment chain, which are costly to resolve and often require intervention from customer service representatives.

The ClearCommerce Enterprise Merchant Engine then implements the rules for automatic fraud protection. This includes validating the card number, checking the billing address, searching through customer history data to look for fraud patterns and to prevent duplicate orders.

The system alerts the accounting and fulfilment platforms that an order has been placed and accepted for shipment and that credit/debit card settlement can now take place. This entire procedure is conducted in real time and the engine is scalable to enable multiple transactions to be processed on one server.

A healthy future with ClearCommerce

Figgitt concluded: 'Thanks to ClearCommerce, we are now effectively servicing our loyal customers without making them feel like criminals and at the same time identifying and eliminating fraudsters.'

For further information contact: Alan Scutt, ClearCommerce Europe, Tel: +44 (0)1784 430 200; Fax: +44 (0)1784 430 201; Email: ascutt@clearcommerce.com.

Corporate profile: Proseq

Do not ask for just an Internet service, ask for a secure Internet service, writes Arnt W K Brox, Managing Director of Proseq.

In an increasingly uncertain world there's one thing that you can be sure of – someone, somewhere is abusing your network or the services that are key to your business, be it on the Internet or on a private network.

Of course, network abuse and hacking can come in a variety of forms. On one hand, your customers could be participating in activities deemed illegal under your own Service Level Agreement (SLA). Then, on the other hand, there could be incidents of spamming, portscanning and hacking against your customers.

Whichever way you look at it, someone is trying to undermine your business. And that can mean only one thing – an erosion of your bottom-line profit.

This is where Proseq comes in – with a raft of world class services that can help to improve operating profit and restore investor confidence. Our unique portfolio of security monitoring and management services can be configured to meet your – and your customers' – precise needs, and is available through key international and UK service providers. Proseq services are available in the UK through partners such as Morse and Telenor Business Solutions UK.

What do we do?

In a nutshell, our partners either integrate our service to provide secure Internet services, or they provide unique security services with the required level of local support.

We pride ourselves on having a round-the-clock operating centre with competence and vigilance to help and guide our customers through everything from small everyday incidents to serious attacks.

Because our staff have years of collective Internet security experience, we appreciate that each customer has their own way of working and their own established procedures and systems. Therefore, we adopt a policy that we call 'dynamic integration'. This means that, no matter how much or how little you need to outsource your own abuse management systems, Proseq is on hand to integrate its own operations with yours – dovetailing our own expertise with your preferred working practices.

How do we do it?

Our partners provide our customers with everything from simple standardised security monitoring and handling SLAs to bespoke SLAs, integrating data and sensors from a variety of sources, and not only the standard intrusion detection systems (IDSs).

Our partners and Proseq focus on what level of risk customers want to handle, and then select the technology required to reach the required level of risk control. There is still far too much focus on technology out there, and we are still seeing a lot of discussion about the selection of specific IDS technologies, rather than the appropriate level of risk handling for customer information and data. Giving the right level of SLA to facilitate the right level of risk handling is our goal.

The SLAs provided through our partners are, therefore, aimed at market segments and customer requirements, in contrast to the number of IDS sensors etc. We provide:

■ microIDS services – aimed at detecting and handling attacks and intrusions for customers with lower risk levels and less complex Internet access or services. They may be SMEs, but may also be larger customers with fewer requirements.
■ WISE services – bespoke SLAs for customers with higher risk requirements and larger networks or more complex Internet services, either internal or external.
■ abuse services – detection and handling of abuse of data, information or systems and networks.
■ quality of service and security services – it is key to security and operations that the service that handles your key information is functional. Therefore we also offer services that monitor, detect and alert in terms of the functionality of these services.

The bottom line

Of course, network abuse management isn't just for fun. One of the worst things for any customer is to see its services being unavailable, or to see capacity being eroded through no fault of their own.

MicroIDS is targeted at organisations of any size that are dependent on the Internet for business, as well as those companies that may already be considering an intrusion detection solution but are discouraged by the complexity and cost of those currently on offer. MicroIDS also provides users with an ideal opportunity to evaluate a leading-edge managed network security service without incurring the cost and service risks normally associated with this route.

Because network intrusion, denial of service attacks and even website defacement can be disastrous for virtually any organisation, Proseq offers a range of managed security services (MSS) that can be fully integrated with an organisation's own network management procedures, guaranteeing the best possible defence against external hacker attacks as well as possible internal threats. By using Proseq's managed solution, companies can benefit from superior economies of scale without setting up round-the-clock security operations.

Additionally, this approach enables organisations to take advantage of the cost savings inherent in not needing to buy in expertise that would not be available in-house. This allows organisations to receive superior protection and better standards of support and service to ensure the risks and incidents are handled.

Issues of intranet and Internet security have become increasingly important, as companies continue to adopt network-based solutions. Inevitably, the need to focus operations around such an environment leaves organisations potentially exposed to malicious attacks. In response to this Proseq's latest initiative provides a totally managed solution that enables organisations to concentrate on core business without having to worry about securing their operations against unwanted intrusions.

ISPs (Internet service providers) offering always-on services, such as broadband cable or ADSL, invite particular risk. Any reduction in overall network capacity can have a devastating effect on available bandwidth. Traditionally, the only way out has been to lease more capacity at horrendous expense or – probably even worse – fall back on your minimum capacity promises.

Proseq's Active Abuse Management service enables us to police an ISP's SLA, and take appropriate enforcement action against end-users that contravene its provisions. What is termed appropriate action will be agreed with the ISP beforehand, and may include a warning, a recommendation to subscribe to an alternative product offering, or even removal from the ISP's customer list.

Active Abuse Management is ideal for:

■ monitoring peer-to-peer services and server activity;
■ monitoring mail and usenet spamming;
■ detection of excessive portscanning;
■ detection of other Internet occurrences that could require active handling – including events like the Code Red worm;
■ abuse handling.

Vulnerability update and testing service

Our well-established Vulnerability Update and Testing Service provides customers with the very latest information on all known vulnerability discoveries, and will even advise you when new patches become available. Vulnerability testing may be integrated in our security monitoring SLAs, provided as separate SLAs performed at pre-defined intervals or as stand-alone projects.

Our centre of excellence and our partners

Naturally, while we make good use of our state-of-the-art software and hardware facilities, the one thing that we have become famous for is our highly trained and dedicated personnel. In fact, quite apart from our unique blend of optimised software solutions, Proseq's team of white-coat security analysts, located at our Centre of Excellence in Norway, is one of the main reasons that we stand head & shoulders above the competition.

Thanks to the special bond that our analysts have with all our customers and partners, we can offer customers a whole series of tangible benefits – ranging from flexibility and independence, right through to security and local experience. Each of which is desirable on its own but, when combined, make an unbeatable combination.

For further information contact: Proseq AS, Nygata 4 (Postal address: P.O. box 618), N-4841 Arendal, Norway. Tel: +47 37 70 98 00; Fax: +47 37 70 98 01; Website:www.proseq.net/abuse

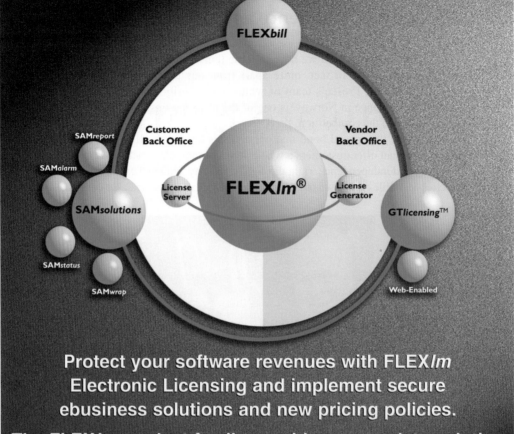

Software protection

Cost effective, robust security? The answer is straightforward.

Straightforward Advice

Centrinet have compiled a portfolio of best of breed security products, all of which are proven in the most demanding of enterprises.

For straightforward security advice based on your business needs contact our dedicated account team.

Straightforward Pricing

Are you tired of complex, expensive quotations? At Centrinet we believe in straightforward competitive prices without hidden extras.

Straightforward Results

Centrinet currently manage effective, robust solutions in over 40 countries to thousands of end user organisations.

Call 01522 559600 email info@centri.net or click onto www.centri.net

"Centrinet have been a key player in supporting Regus's IT services to its customers"

Mike Brockington - CIO, Global IT Operations and Telecoms,

Regus Business Centres plc

Centrinet, Straightforward Security

Check Point
Solution Partner
Premier
Managed Service
Provider

Centrinet Limited, Witham Park House, Waterside South, Lincoln, Lincolnshire, LN5 7JN

Intrusion detection

Intrusion detection systems (IDS) are a vital part of any information security policy, but they do need careful management, writes Stuart Eaton from Centrinet.

IDS acceptance as a recognised component to security

A common analogy applied to intrusion detection systems and firewalls is that of your home. Suppose that you move into a new home in an affluent area. After a year you pick up the local paper, the headline tells you of a spate of burglaries and vandalism in the area, targeting your prosperous well-advertised housing estate. Upon reading this you ensure that you have a strong front door and put a couple of extra locks on. A week later, entering the front room you are greeted by the sight of broken glass and no television. So what happened? Although the door was perfectly secure, the thieves simply smashed the kitchen window, climbed through and helped themselves.

It is common practice for people to buy an alarm or even a dog to complement the locks and doors of a house. The reasoning behind this is obvious: they give you an early warning of an attack on your property and they also provide a deterrent to the would-be thief when their use is detected. How many times have we read stories of reformed criminals talking about targeting the 'easy' house without the alarm or dog? The contemporary internet security landscape is increasingly mirroring our domestic analogy.

IDS is not 'fire and forget'

Intrusion detection, above perhaps any other security measure, cannot be thought of as 'fire and forget'. The threats faced by security staff change day by day and the IDS should be updated correspondingly. There are two key points to remember regarding intrusion detection:

1. It does not assess and anticipate vulnerabilities in the network so much as monitor those areas of the network that administrators believe are vulnerable.
2. It does not automatically protect and secure a network once it detects an attack.

These points illustrate the industry reasoning that a well-deployed IDS solution should have a fully trained security specialist administering the solution as a key component.

An IDS solution is only as effective as the tuning and signature files. A solution that creates too many false alerts or false positives will undermine the credibility of the IDS within the business, and can often lead to staff simply switching it off or at least ignoring its output.

A solution that creates too few alerts can lead to a false sense of security and ultimately should lead you to believe that your system is not detecting enough suspicious traffic. This is especially pertinent when coupled with the findings detailed within the Honeynet project.

The Honeynet project involved servers attached to the Internet acting as decoys; this then lured potential hackers in order to monitor their activities and methods of gaining entry. The findings from this project were then documented and used to make people aware of the potential threats. One of the most startling facts was that the quickest time a system was compromised was 15 minutes; the average was 72 hours.

The nature of the Internet and Internet-borne attacks is that of an ever-changing 24/7/365 evolving entity. Your IDS solution and the people that administer it should have the tools and the skills to ensure that you can keep pace and also evolve securely.

IDS should be part of your reaction to the threat

Compaq estimate that the average financial trading house can lose £300,000–400,000 in an hour of downtime; further to this, the average large company loses US$20,000 per hour during the first 72 hours of its response to a security breach, according to a recent study by Gartner.[1]

These alarming figures should lead us to ensure that our companies at least adhere to minimum measures to help diminish the threat to business. These measures include the following:

- Switch on audit logs for all key servers – when efficiently and effectively configured, these logs will provide adequate information to identify and investigate any problems.
- Implement properly designed firewalls – these can track all traffic in and out of the site, logging and inspecting every packet of information to ensure its legitimacy.
- Install intrusion detection software – if properly configured, this software will quickly identify known patterns of attack and immediately shut out the attacker only, while sounding the appropriate alarms.

---

[1] 'Estimating loss from infrastructure compromise', Gartner.

- Hire the right people – make sure your technical personnel completely understand the issues, the technologies and the solutions. Otherwise consider outsourcing.
- Test defences regularly – the rapid rate of change in both the technology area and the hacking community means that you must test your own defences on a regular basis.
- Design the network to isolate attacks – if the worst happens and the hacker gets inside, appropriate network configuration, firewalls and other tools will ensure any damage the hacker could cause is isolated to a small area.
- Have an incident response plan – identifying, reacting and resolving the problem immediately is the real business dilemma. Most organisations implement the right preventative measures but do not prepare and train for the worst.
- Focus on preventative measures – swift, large-volume, automated attacks require sophisticated, automated defence mechanisms. Identifying a problem an hour after it occurs and then trying to trace and resolve it is not an option.
- Keep all software up-to-date – implementing all security fixes and patches as they are released will go a long way to reducing your vulnerability to these attacks.

Management by specialists

The nature of intrusion detection integrates with the 'managed security' model to a greater extent than perhaps any other security technology. *Network Computing* noted,[2] 'The case for outsourcing some of this IDS pain is getting more and more compelling.' The characteristics of IDS output require skilled technicians around the clock to address the alerts. The infrastructure however must be in place to allow effective interpretation of the alerts and must be able to scale to the number of alerts generated during attacks. This is a point ratified by the Sysadmin, Audit, Network, Security (SANS) Institute: 'It has become a middleware[3] nightmare to manage the outputs from IDSs. Monitoring and analysing alerts from even a handful of IDSs can quickly overwhelm security staff.'

Intrusion detection should be a technology explored by any company that is serious about the threat inherent in today's connected business world. The decision to outsource this function, whilst compelling, should not be taken lightly.

Centrinet are a leading provider of Internet and network security solutions based on the innovative use of the best products and services. Our passion for customer service and technical excellence, combined with a no-nonsense approach to business, provides our clients with a refreshing and unique experience.

For further information contact: Centrinet Limited, Witham Park House, Waterside South, Lincoln, Lincolnshire, LN5 7JN. Tel: +44 (0)1522 559 600; Fax: +44 (0)1522 533 745; Email: enquiries@centri.net; Webite: www.centri.net

---

[2] *Network Computing,* 'To Catch a Thief', 20 August 2001.
[3] Middleware is software that connects two otherwise separate applications.

3.2

Firewalls

Firewalls can block traffic and hide your network from the outside world. Stuart Eaton from Centrinet explains the three technologies involved.

A firewall can be a piece of software, hardware, or a mixture of both, that enforces an access control policy between networks – for example between the private corporate network and the public Internet. A widely used analogy for a firewall is that of a lock on a door, although in reality a firewall offers far more flexibility. A firewall can block traffic, but it can also hide your network from the outside world and screen outgoing traffic. A firewall is an essential and minimum component in any Internet security strategy. Firewall technologies broadly fall into three categories: packet filter, application-level proxy server and stateful. We will discuss these three technologies below and list the most popular firewalls in each category.

Packet filter

A packet filter is the most basic type of firewall and is often free and available on popular routers. A packet filter simply checks the IP address of incoming traffic against an access control list (ACL), and will deny access to addresses that don't correspond to this list. Packet filters can also have rules based on data type or TCP/IP (transmission control protocol/Internet protocol) port numbers.

Packet filters are often very fast and very cheap; however they are susceptible to IP spoofing. IP spoofing is a technique whereby an external address will 'pretend' to come from a trusted source, thereby defeating the rule base of the packet filter and gaining access to the network. Popular packet filters are Linux's 'ipchains'; OpenBSD's 'pf' and FreeBSD's 'ipfw'.

Application proxy

The second firewall technology is known as an 'application proxy firewall'. An application proxy firewall uses software to intercept connections and examines the application used for each individual packet[1] to verify its authenticity.

Application-level firewall technology checks for permission to connect to another network and can enforce access control rules specific to the application. Each application has its own proxy program that emulates the application's protocol – for example, FTP (file transfer protocol) for file transfers, HTTP (hypertext transfer protocol) for the Internet and SMTP/POP3 (simple mail transfer protocol/post office protocol, version 3.0) for email.

Whilst proxy firewalls are considered to be very secure the processing overhead can lead to degradation in performance. Popular proxy firewalls are 'WatchGuard'and NAI's 'Gauntlet'.

Stateful firewalls

Stateful inspection is a technology developed and patented by Check Point Technologies, a leading provider of software firewalls.

Stateful inspection is an architecture that works at the network layer. Unlike packet filtering, which examines a packet based solely on the information in its header, stateful inspection tracks each connection and makes sure they are valid. A stateful firewall may examine not just the header information but also the contents of the packet in order to determine packet information further than simply source and destination.

A stateful inspection firewall monitors the state of the connection and compiles this information in a dynamic-state table. Because of this, filtering decisions are based not only on IP address rules but also on behaviour that has been established by prior packets that have passed through the firewall. Stateful firewalls will also drop connections should they attempt an action that is not a standard use of the protocol. Popular stateful firewalls are 'Cisco PIX' and 'Check Point'.

Centrinet are a leading provider of Internet and network security solutions based on the innovative use of the best products and services. Our passion for customer service and technical excellence, combined with a no-nonsense approach to business, provides our clients with a refreshing and unique experience.

For further information contact: Centrinet Limited, Witham Park House, Waterside South, Lincoln, Lincolnshire, LN5 7JN. Tel: +44 (0)1522 559 600; Fax: +44 (0)1522 533 745; Email: enquiries@centri.net; Webite: www.centri.net

---

[1] A unit of data formatted for transmission on a network.

Virus attack

Viruses can do irreparable damage. With the right safeguards this can be easily avoided, says Natasha Staley at Sophos.

As too many organisations are aware, virus infections can be both destructive and far-reaching. Nowadays it would be difficult to find a company whose everyday routine does not rely upon the smooth running of its IT infrastructure. It is therefore easy to see why a rather unpleasant can of worms is opened when that is compromised.

The nature of the virus threat

Damage to data

One of the most talked about effects of a virus attack is the damage it can do to a company's data. Many viruses are capable of wiping hard disks or corrupting the records held on a machine. Worse still are those viruses known as 'data diddlers', which subtly alter the figures in a spreadsheet or words within a document. Because the changes they make are not immediately obvious it can be weeks or even months before anyone notices that something is amiss. By that time the damage can be impossible to undo as back-ups are corrupted as well. That said, if a company does fall foul of a virus that simply eliminates data, back-ups can often be used to restore the lost information.

Clean-up costs

Deciphering how much it costs an organisation to reinstate lost data, or to negate corruptions made by malicious code is an almost impossible task and depends greatly on the specifics of the virus in question. However, in most cases the IT department will be called in to perform the clean-up operation whilst the everyday running of the company has to be put on hold. This could mean that email is disrupted, a website becomes unusable and staff within the organisation are unable to perform their usual tasks. In a worst-case scenario it could mean bringing in an external party to help. As alarming as all of this sounds, data destruction is far from the worst thing a virus can do.

Spreading the infection

There are some viruses, such as Melissa and Sircam, that are capable of randomly selecting documents from an infected PC and distributing them to the contacts listed in an infected user's address book. The virus will not search for any document in particular – whether it happens upon your latest financial projections or your plans to merge with another company is really left to chance. The likelihood, though, is that if it is a document of that nature, there are certain people (quite possibly in your email contact list) whom you wouldn't want to see it.

A virus that sends out potentially sensitive information about a company can put it in a rather awkward position. Not only can a leak place competitors at an advantage, but suppliers, business partners and customers are also likely to find out that a business has allowed its security to be compromised by a virus. This can damage the trust of one company in another, as security is still very much a taboo issue. It can also make the parties that deal with a company feel vulnerable about the information they hold relating to them.

Unfortunately, this kind of situation is not something that can be rectified easily. Building relationships and a credible reputation can often take years and yet can be practically wiped out in a matter of minutes. Re-establishing relationships and reputation is far from an overnight task, and, in some cases, they could be irreparably damaged.

Protecting against viruses

However, it is not all doom and gloom. Virus infection is by no means inevitable for any company and the good news is that it is possible to protect corporate networks fairly easily.

Anti-virus software

Probably the most obvious step to take is to install a reliable anti-virus solution that is updated regularly. Most anti-virus solutions are able to detect the majority of viruses; but the speed with which updates to protect against the latest viruses are delivered differs somewhat. Most vendors offer automated updating over the Internet but customers should check out exactly how often they will be updated.

Policy solutions

Apart from the software there are other measures a company can take to protect itself against malicious code. One of these is to develop a safe computing policy whereby employees are informed of how to use their machines safely. Educating users about possible threats should begin at company induction stage so that members of staff know what is expected of them from the outset. It is astounding how many companies do not do this. You wouldn't let someone drive around the M25 without a licence and yet people are placed in front of PCs and are expected to know how to use them correctly.

A safe computing policy should include points such as not opening unexpected emails and not downloading material from the Internet. The vast majority of viruses are spread via the Internet and email, which is why this is so important. Even if an email is received from a known source it could still be infected, so it is worth questioning whether it was expected and whether it is in the apparent sender's usual style. Many virus writers use extremely bad spelling and grammar, which can be an obvious clue as to what the email really contains. An email from a known associate in a foreign language should also set the alarm bells ringing!

In addition, no files with double extensions should be executed. There are very few occasions when such a file would be legitimately required and the vast majority of them should be treated with suspicion. The simplest thing to do is to ask the sender to re-send the file with the correct extension.

Another measure to include within such a policy is the saving of Word documents as rich text format (.rtf) instead of as documents (.doc). Docs support the macro language, which allows macro viruses to run – it is far more difficult to infect an .rtf file. Users should also be instructed not to open or forward joke, movie or graphics files. Although these file-types are virtually unable to support viruses, malicious code can be disguised as a file of this type.

System procedures

Network administrators should also employ measures such as disabling Windows Scripting Host, changing the CMOS boot-up sequence and blocking certain file-types at the email gateway. Some vendors include technology within their products that allows IT managers to prevent certain files from ever entering an organisation – this is certainly something to look out for when purchasing an anti-virus solution. A full list of safe computing procedures that would form a good basis for such a policy can be found at www.sophos.com/safe-computing.

Appropriate responses

Another important issue for organisations to consider once a safe computing policy is in place is what to do should an employee contradict the guidelines and allow a virus to penetrate the company defences. The natural inclination of some businesses would be to punish the member of staff concerned, either by verbal or written warning or by dismissal. However, this is often not the most effective way of dealing with such a situation. If staff know that they face disciplinary measures should they be responsible for a virus infection then they are far more likely to attempt to cover up an incident, which makes it far harder to administer the clean-up once it does come to light. Ideally in that situation an employee should feel comfortable with coming forward and admitting that they have made a mistake. Only if they continue to ignore the guidelines should users be disciplined.

Defending an organisation against malicious code of all types is not the sole responsibility of the IT department – every employee plays a part in protecting a company. The measures that are put in place do not have to be complicated, and if staff are encouraged to follow them from the outset they should become second nature.

Conclusions

Anti-virus protection in today's climate demands a multi-faceted approach. Gone are the days when simply installing the software was enough. That software needs to be maintained constantly, by vendor and customer, to ensure that it detects the maximum number of viruses. In addition to the software, all users within an organisation should be taught how to use their computers safely. They may not be able to have as much fun as they once did, but a workable balance between functionality and security has to be sought.

Despite the horror stories of what viruses can do, it is worth remembering that it is possible to mount a comprehensive defence. Most virus incidents can be avoided relatively easily. The key to ensuring that an organisation remains virus-free is constant vigilance and attention. That may sound intimidating, but in view of the potential consequences of infection it is a small price to pay.

Sophos, the Real Business/CBI Growing Business Awards Company of the Year, is a world leader in anti-virus protection. It is strongly focused on the corporate marketplace where its vision, commitment to research and development, and rigorous attention to quality have taken it from strength to strength.

Sophos's increasingly rapid growth internationally is reflected in a user base of well over 20 million and revenues that soared by nearly 50 per cent in the period 2001–2002. Sophos products are sold and supported in over 150 countries through a global network of subsidiaries and partners. In a field where virus numbers typically rise by up to 800 per month, Sophos's foresight and innovative approach have kept it at the forefront of the market.

For further information contact: Natasha Staley, Anti-Virus Consultant, Sophos Anti-Virus, The Pentagon, Abingdon Science Park, Abingdon, Oxfordshire OX14 3YP. Tel: +44 (0)1235 559 933; Fax: +44 (0) 1235 544 114; Email: natasha.staley@sophos.com; Website: www.sophos.com

Authentication and encryption

Positively determine with just whom you are doing business, writes Tim Pickard from RSA Security.

Reports of hackers accessing popular e-business websites and flaunting customer credit card numbers are well known and increasingly common, to the point that they have become every e-business's worst PR and legal nightmare. With business-to-consumer (B2C) e-commerce expected to reach US$108 billion by 2003, and business-to-business (B2B) e-commerce expected to increase to US$1 trillion over the same period, the need for electronic security has never been more evident. The key to this security is authentication: that is, positively determining with whom you're doing business.

E-business 'pressure'

The Internet has revolutionised business with staggering results. This has placed tremendous pressure on companies to quickly establish a presence in the potentially lucrative e-world or risk failure. Unfortunately, with time-to-market being such a critical requirement, the basic approach to launching an e-business is too often of the form: 'ready, fire, aim'. As a result, e-businesses sometimes pay less attention to implementing the necessary policies and mechanisms that would result in a trusted and secure e-business environment.

Inevitably, certain parties have sought to take advantage of this negligence. 'Trojan horse' computer viruses that steal passwords; competitors accessing seemingly protected databases using borrowed passwords of acquaintances; personal accounts being exposed to every member of a bank: none of these examples are just threats anymore; they are reality – and it's not just sophisticated computer hackers who are causing the problems. Thrill-seeking teenagers, novice computer programmers trying to make a name for themselves, and criminal organisations are all using password-cracking tools that are readily available on the Internet. As new e-business models become more complex and attackers develop more sophisticated tools, we can only expect the number of security breaches to increase.

At the same time, it is important to remember that the essence of e-business is that transactions occur between people who are represented by machines. The anonymity of these transactions makes it more difficult to identify the parties involved and therefore to ensure a trusted business relationship. Since all successful business relationships are based on trust, establishing online trust should be one of the primary goals of any e-business. Data privacy, data integrity and user authorisation are all essential elements of e-security. But the real cornerstone of e-business trust is authentication. This chapter explains how each of these contributes to a successful e-business strategy.

The keys to securing your e-business

Secure e-business can be broken down into four areas:

1. **Authentication** – ensuring that both the sender and recipient are who they say they are;
2. **Data privacy** – guaranteeing the confidentiality of information as it moves around the public Internet;
3. **Data integrity** – ensuring that authenticated users in a transaction are not able to deny actions they have taken;
4. **Authorisation** – denying unauthorised users access to information they're not supposed to see.

Authentication

This is the cornerstone of e-business security, and is defined as positively identifying and proving the authenticity of those with whom you're doing business. Without authentication other security measures that you put in place can be ineffective.

Passwords aren't enough

Today, requiring a username and password is the most common technique for authenticating a user. On the surface this single factor (something a user knows) may appear to be an adequate solution. After all, there are roughly 2.8 trillion possibilities for an eight-character password composed of random alphanumeric characters. But because we all tend to choose passwords that are short and easy to remember – such as important dates or names of family members – our passwords tend to be relatively easy for others to guess, steal or crack. Social engineering also contributes to the unreliable nature of passwords.

Another problem is that your username and password may not be protected as they travel across the Internet. For example, a typical web server's basic HTTP authentication system, used on many websites, does not encrypt the username or password. And unencrypted passwords are extremely susceptible to interception by hackers who are 'sniffing' for them. The bottom line is that you need stronger authentication to create and maintain a trusted environment for e-business.

Levels of authentication

Varying levels of authentication strength exist, and your choice will be based on the value or sensitivity of the information that you're protecting, balanced against other considerations like usability, deployment, and budget.

Passwords are the weakest, although most widely used, form of authentication. They help to identify users by requiring a single factor of identification: their secret code. This method of authentication is perceived to be easy to deploy and inexpensive. However, history has proven that these codes are easily guessed, stolen or otherwise compromised and are not as easy or inexpensive to maintain as one might think. Surprisingly, passwords are one of the most ineffective forms of authentication.

The use of *digital certificates* as a form of authentication is becoming more widespread with the growth of Internet transactions. Alone or protected with a password, certificates help identify users by requiring access to digital credentials that should only be used by the rightful owner. However, the relative strength of digital certificates as an authentication solution depends on how securely they are protected. For example, digital certificates stored insecurely on a hard drive can be likened to your wallet left open on your desk.

Digital certificates gain strength when they are accompanied by a *controlled password policy*. Here, a trusted 'certificate authority' issues certificates that verify the digital identity of users' private keys. Adding a public key infrastructure with a centrally managed certificate policy statement that establishes password requirements (ie every password has to be nine alphanumeric characters in length) can improve the strength of certificates as a form of user authentication.

Two-factor authentication is much stronger than password security or unprotected certificates because it requires users to present two forms of identification before gaining access to protected resources. Similar to using a bank ATM, users must both know their PIN and possess their authentication device (token or smart card). The combination proves that users are who they say they are.

Combining *two-factor authentication* and *digital certificates* enhances the strength of your authentication services dramatically. Often, digital certificates are stored insecurely so anyone can assume the identities of your users. By requiring two forms of identification to access credentials, you are able to bind users' digital identities to their physical identities, which allows you to be more confident that users are who they say they are.

Introducing *smartcards* to protect *digital certificates* is one of the strongest levels of authentication service. Not only is access to the smartcard protected with two-factor authentication, but certificates/key pairs can also be generated and stored on the smartcard. In fact, the private key never leaves the card, so it can never be accessed by unauthorised users or copied to a server.

By adding a third factor – such as *biometrics* – to the above, you can achieve the strongest available level of authentication. Biometrics refers to a characteristic that is unique to a user. This measurement can be achieved through fingerprinting, retinal scanning and voice-printing. This third authentication factor when combined with certificates stored on a smartcard is impenetrable.

Data privacy

Sensitive information needs to be protected while it is moving from point to point across the Internet. For example, you don't want competitors to be able to grab a copy of a proposal when you email it to a prospective customer. And you probably want to protect usernames and passwords – and of course credit card numbers – that accompany transmissions.

Most web browsers have built-in 'secure sockets layer' (SSL) capabilities to ensure the privacy of information that is transferred between a Web server and a user's Web browser. This is done by encrypting, or scrambling, information before sending it and then decrypting it at the receiving end, making it virtually impossible for the transaction to be translated if intercepted. That means the transaction is private, which is crucial in e-business.

Data integrity

It is also important that neither party is able to declare that a transaction never took place or that the received data was somehow different from that transmitted. For example, if you receive a large online order from one of your resellers can you really be sure that it's legitimate? What happens if you deliver the order and they claim that the order they placed was significantly smaller? Or they deny having placed it at all?

For non-repudiation you need to be able to prove that the sender and receiver are who they say they are and that the transaction has not been altered. This can be accomplished by using client-side digital certificates that authenticate a transaction – thus proving that the transaction has not been altered during transmission. It should be noted, however, that you still need to prove that users are who they say they are – ie not disgruntled employees or thrill-seeking teens – to make them accountable for the transaction. Only two-factor authentication can definitively bind a user's physical identity to their digital identity.

Authorisation

Different users need access to different types of information, and it's important to prevent unauthorised users from seeing that information. For example, your HR staff needs to be able to view and update the employee database, but other employees and contractors should not be looking at your salary. Your sales channel needs access to the latest product information, development schedules and pricing, but that internal information isn't usually something that you want competitors to see.

Authorisation involves restricting user access to machines, directories, files, and application programs. There are several levels of authorisation. The first involves limiting access at the URL level to protect machines and their contents. The second provides conditional access to directories and files based on access control lists, and the third involves elaborate rule-based access control. In any of its forms, authorisation helps you enforce data access rules once a user reaches protected resources.

Identity management

Authentication is therefore – amongst these other security measures – critical to the success of your e-business initiative. Another considerable threat, however, lies in the staggering proliferation of identities on the Internet. Hundreds of millions of people around the world now use the Internet daily at home and at work, encountering myriad corporate applications, e-business interfaces and web services. Many of these applications require a unique user name and, as a result, an individual will typically possess not one but several digital identities.

Additionally, digital identities are not perpetual: they are created for new employees, and when those employees leave their digital identity expires – or should expire – as of their termination date. An employee moving from one part of an organisation to another, or being promoted to a higher management level, may need to have updated access rights and other information attached to his or her digital identity.

Therefore companies need to be able to trust the identities of users who seek to access their Internet-based resources. Further, they need to manage and control authorised identities to ensure they are current and being used in accordance with established policies. For this reason, organisations need to assess their own identity management needs, engage in detailed discussions with business partners about their needs and plans, and explore in conjunction with a reliable vendor how to implement and integrate such a solution into their IT environments.

An open standard for identity management – including authentication, single sign-on and web access management capabilities – will help businesses lower costs, accelerate commercial opportunities and increase user productivity and customer satisfaction.

Initiatives such as the Liberty Alliance demonstrate how companies are already working together to make e-business easier without compromising credential details. For example, it will soon be possible to organise your complete holiday logistics – rent a villa, book flights and hire a car – in a single online transaction, by authenticating *once* and then moving freely between affiliated websites without having to repeatedly re-enter your details.

A federated approach will bring substantial benefits to users and businesses alike. Online transactions are often abandoned, and users have identified the need to complete and often re-complete forms as being the single biggest reason for this; clearly this is a major obstacle to e-commerce. Within an identity management system, users will appreciate:

■ the convenience of a single identity and authentication for a wide range of resources, applications and websites;
■ the ability to specify under what conditions certain pieces of information can and cannot be shared; and
■ policies and standards on data storage, usage and sharing designed to protect their privacy and prevent fraud and identity theft.

In turn, businesses will benefit by being able to:

■ trust the identities of employees, partners and customers;
■ receive pre-authenticated users from business partners' sites; and
■ introduce new services and identify new business opportunities.

Conclusion

None of this is possible without the core foundation of e-security: strong user authentication. Once this is in place, the rest – mitigated network security risk, reduced costs, increased revenues, protected investments and greater compliance – will follow, and companies will be positioned to deal securely, conveniently and *profitably* over the Internet.

Tim Pickard is EMEA Strategic Marketing Director at RSA Security. RSA Security is the most trusted name in e-security, helping organisations to build secure, trusted foundations for e-business through its two-factor authentication, web access management, encryption and public key management systems. A truly global company with more than 8,000 customers, RSA Security is renowned for providing technologies that help organisations conduct e-business with confidence.

For further information contact: RSA UK, Ireland and EMEA Sales, RSA House, Western Road, Bracknell, Berks RG12 1RT. Tel: +44 (0)1344 781000; Fax: + 44 (0)1344 781010.

Digital signatures

There is nothing complicated about digital signatures – they simply act as a means of verification. However, the ramifications of this can be far-reaching, writes Bart Vansevenant, at GlobalSign.

The potential of business opportunities and enhanced customer convenience services offered by the Internet is phenomenal. From home banking to network shopping and online information subscription services, security remains a growing concern. Key questions that are asked include:

- How do I know that the other party is indeed the person or organisation that he or she claims to be?
- Can I be sure that nobody can read the communication or transaction that travels over the Internet?
- Can I be sure that nobody can change the information that I send electronically?
- As a business, can I be sure that a customer that deals with me electronically cannot deny its online transactions?

Digital certificates and *digital signatures* can answer these important questions and thus secure communications, transactions and access control.

What are digital signatures?

Like the signature you use on written documents, digital signatures are now being used to identify authors and co-signers of email or electronic data. Digital signatures are created and verified using digital certificates. To understand what digital certificates are we need to take a closer look at 'cryptography'. Cryptography is the science of transforming information you can read (in plain text) into information someone else cannot read. In this process information is coded (encryption) to stop information from being read or altered by anyone but the intended recipient. It may be intercepted, but it will not be intelligible to someone without the ability to decode (decryption) the message. Encryption and decryption require both a mathematical formula (or 'algorithm') to convert data between readable and encoded formats and a key.

There are two types of cryptography: symmetric (or 'secret key') and asymmetric (or 'public key'). Symmetric key cryptography is characterised by the fact that the same key used to encrypt the data is used to decrypt the data. Clearly, this key must be kept secret among the communicating parties, otherwise the communication can be intercepted and decrypted by others. Until the mid-1970s, symmetric cryptography was the only form of cryptography available, so the same secret had to be known by all individuals participating in any application that provided a security service. However, this all changed when Whitfield Diffie and Martin Hellman introduced the notion of 'public key cryptography' in 1976.

Digital signatures use public key cryptography. In such a system two keys are required in order for two parties to exchange information in a secure fashion: a public key and a private key. If one key is used to encrypt a message, then only the other key in the pair can be used to decrypt it. Although the keys of the public and private key pair are mathematically related, it is computationally infeasible to derive one key from the other, so the private key is protected from duplication or forgery even when someone knows the public key. Therefore it is safe to openly distribute your public key for everyone to use, but it is essential that your private key remains closely guarded and secret. The public key can be used to verify a message signed with the private key or to encrypt messages that can only be decrypted using the private key. If someone wants to send you an encrypted message, they encrypt the message with your public key so that you, being the sole possessor of the corresponding private key of the pair, are the only one who can decrypt it.

How are digital signatures created and verified?

To create a digital signature, the signer creates a 'hash' – an algorithm that creates a unique shortened version of the message – and then uses his/her private key to encrypt the hash. The encrypted hash is the digital signature. If the message were changed in any way, the hash-result of the changed message would be different. The digital signature is unique to both the message and the private key used to create it, so it cannot be forged. The digital signature is then appended to the message and both are sent to the message recipient. The recipient recreates the hash from the received message, and then uses the public key of the original sender to decrypt the hash included in the received message. If the two hash results are identical, two things have been verified:

1. The digital signature was created using the signer's private key (assurance that the public key corresponds to the signer's private key) – no one is pretending to be or masquerading as the signer. This verifies the *authenticity* of the signer, and the signer cannot claim not to have signed the message.
2. The message has not been changed. This verifies the *integrity* of the message.

The role of a certification authority (CA)

A digital signature is created using a digital certificate, which binds a public key to an individual or organisation. The binding of a public key to an individual or organisation is certified by a trusted source, typically a certification authority (CA). A CA is a trusted authority that issues and manages digital certificates. A CA uses a public key infrastructure (PKI) to perform the life-cycle management of digital certificates. These certificates typically include the owner's public key, the expiration date of the certificate, the owner's name and other information about the public key owner. CAs may also be involved in a number of administrative tasks such as end-user registration, but these are often delegated to the registration authority (RA). The role of the RA is to verify the identity of the person or organisation that attempts to register.

Who can use digital signatures?

Basically anyone who makes transactions over the Internet and wants those to be secured. If you are an employee of a company that has a website/network with restricted access, then you will probably need a digital certificate to authenticate yourself on this website. You're tired of queuing in a bank? You want to do home banking? Then you also need a certificate to authenticate yourself. You are developing ActiveX or Java applets? Then you need a certificate to digitally sign your applet and have people trust it! You're using your email to send sensitive data over the Internet? Then you definitely need a certificate to sign and encrypt your messages.

Legal framework

Digital signatures can be compared to the traditional handwritten signature that has been used for centuries to do business. The only difference is that the transactions take place via a new medium, namely the Internet. Therefore new laws have to be implemented to reflect this new reality.

The use of digital signatures is supported by recent legislative actions that provide credibility to the concept of electronic signatures and recognition of the need for such a capability. The US E-Sign Law, passed in 2000, and the EU Digital Signature Law, passed in 2001, are examples of this trend.

Using digital signatures in your business

One of the most crucial questions in any business transaction is the identity of the entity with which the transaction is being conducted. Historically, personal relationships, face-to-face contract signings, notaries and third-party counsel are used to help establish trust in this most important aspect of conducting our business. As the reliance on paper shifts to electronic transactions and documents, so must the reliance on traditional trust factors shift to electronic security measures that authenticate our electronic business partners, customers and suppliers before we engage in the exchange of information, goods and services.

Similarly, the need for confidentiality and confidence in the integrity of exchanged information is critical. Extending this list of security services, there may be further need to establish the non-repudiation of agreements, and to digitally notarise and securely time-stamp transactions.

Digital signatures support all these security services. Let's take a look at some applications in different vertical markets that can benefit from the use of digital signatures:

- **Financial services:** authentication of payment for stock purchases, access control for online banking, digital notarisation of loans;
- **Insurance**: digital signature quotes, authentication of online payment of premiums, version management of documents;
- **Government:** electronic ID-cards (such as the Belgian BelPIC project to provide each citizen with an electronic identity card), automation of electronic response to RFPs, secure messaging within government;
- **Industry**: digital signature of electronic contracts, linking of procurement systems in an automated way, access control for business partner to online applications.

Public key infrastructure (PKI)

When it comes to implementing digital signatures, companies have the choice of:

- using a public CA such as GlobalSign or VeriSign to provide them with digital certificates;
- operating a private CA, meaning that the company will have to purchase and implement its own PKI;
- going for an outsourced PKI solution such as Ubizen OnlineGuardian Certificate Management.

The first alternative is a good solution if, for example, a company wants to provide its employees with digital certificates to sign confidential email communication. If a company wants to deploy certificates across different applications, involving both internal and external parties, or if it wants to be a CA itself, it will have to chose between options 2 and 3. The main parameters related to the decision between these two options are time-to-market, size of population, application, financial and human resources, and legal framework, etc.

For early implementers of PKI, with huge budgets and sufficient IT and administrative capacity, deploying an infrastructure on an in-house basis was most appropriate. However, as PKI attracts increasing interest from a larger number of large and medium-sized companies and organisations, the case for outsourcing PKI becomes favourable. Outsourced PKI solutions provide a multitude of benefits for business. Although the underlying idea is to transfer the burden of implementation and management of the PKI solution to a service provider, there are undoubtedly important strategic and financial advantages in outsourcing trust as well.

GlobalSign is Europe's leading Certificate Service Provider offering digital certificates to individuals and businesses, allowing secure email communication, fully authenticated and confidential e-commerce and trusted software distribution.

GlobalSign's public root key is by default embedded in all major Internet browsers. Consequently, GlobalSign certificates are globally accepted and are not limited by any application, geographic area or business sector. Furthermore GlobalSign is one of the few Certificate Authorities in the world that attained the WebTrust accreditation level.

For further information contact: GlobalSign NV/SA, Philipssite 5, B-3001 Leuven, Belgium. Tel: +32 16 28 74 00; Fax: +32 16 28 74 04; Email: info@globalsign.net; Website: www.globalsign.net

Digital rights

Audio CDs, movie DVDs and Internet downloads are taking security into a new dimension. Simon Mehlman at Macrovision reports on the implications for the ownership of digital data once it is in the hands of the consumer.

The transmission and fair use of information has always been fraught with security issues. From carrier pigeons to the 'Pony Express', the agencies used to carry and deliver information have done so based on two key principles: the rights of confidentiality and the clear expectation of assured delivery. These factors have historically proven to be fundamental to the safe transmission of information. The overriding security issue up to this point in time has been the protection of information *en route* to the intended recipient. Technology has now leaped ahead into a 'digital age'. Whatever the type of content and the form of distribution – from audio CDs to movie DVDs and Internet downloads – a whole new dimension to the issue of security has arisen: the issue of content security and, specifically, the rights and ownership of digital data after it has moved into the domain of the consumer. This is the foundation for digital rights management (DRM).

Digital content is a broad term used to describe the wealth of information and products now available for consumption. From business and entertainment software, to video and Internet feeds, our society has never been so rich in information. The marketplace offers huge rewards to software pirates, from the casual copier to the dedicated hacker, particularly when the cost of a CD burner has fallen to less than €100.

It is no secret that piracy is rife within our society. Many people recognise that piracy of digital content is a criminal offence; however, this does not act as a sufficiently powerful deterrent against people copying music CDs or sharing movies over Internet 'peer to peer' networks like Kazaa. A whole industry has developed around circumventing copy protection, which ranges from selling hardware devices and downloads that remove copy protection to cheap imported DVD players that do not contain required patent licences and thus have a price advantage over legitimate players. It is beyond comprehension that we have laws that allow our own electronics industry to be damaged. Such activities hurt a whole range of interests, including those of the rights holders, the providers of copy protection technology, broadcasters, consumer electronics manufacturers, government tax agencies and consumers.

Content creators can spend a lot of money in research and production. When this content is 'pirated' or subjected to 'illegal home copying', the revenue stream back to the content creators and their publishers can be seriously affected. Digital content can be subject to hacker attacks for a variety of motives, from simply trying to avoid paying for a product, to reverse-engineer coding for competitive product development. The rights and revenues of content owners are being abused, and legislators face the dilemma of how to fairly protect the interested parties.

The goal for content owners for some time has been to develop a range of systems that enforce the rights of copyright owners, whilst at the same time ensuring that the legitimate user is not penalised and does not have their ease of use compromised. It is in nobody's interest to devise a method of copy protection or digital rights management that is effective at the cost of enabling the consumer to enjoy the full benefit and ease of use of the product.

DRM is a term applied to technologies designed to manage rights holders' product. It provides a technology platform to allow trusted packaging, flexible distribution and managed consumption of digital content over Internet protocol (IP) networks. The purpose of DRM is to provide content owners, service providers, distributors and retailers with a safe and secure method for meeting the consumer's need for interactive, on-demand access to movies, online games, books, music and software critical or proprietary data – virtually any type of digital media.

A key aspect of DRM is effective copy management and the presence of a legal structure that protects not only the rights owners but also the rights of technologists and consumer electronic manufacturers. One of the most dubious phrases used in the current legislative process is that of 'copying for non-commercial benefit'. If someone makes a copy of a DVD or TV programme and puts it on the Internet, it may well have been done for non-commercial benefit. However, it is unlikely that the rights owner, who may lose tens of thousand of sales of the product as a result, will feel that they have not suffered a significant commercial loss.

The requirements of rights owners for content protection are varied. A system to protect their content, be it business software or the latest chart-topping music album, must include or provide the following factors:

- a highly secure end-to-end solution;
- seamless interface with existing e-commerce infrastructures;
- scalable architecture to cost-effectively support growing demand;
- no change to existing content authoring workflows;
- media agnostic – usable with any type of compression or file format;
- support for different means of distribution;
- support for flexible business models;
- able to be ported to other devices: STBs, PVR, HMS;
- high-quality user experience.

One key sector, the video industry, has followed a cohesive policy of copy protection involving content owners and consumer electronics manufacturers. By undertaking a range of copy protection initiatives, the amount of revenue lost to illegal copying has been significantly reduced.

As technology has progressed, and we now enjoy our digital content on an increasing number of platforms, the video industry, together with other digital content sectors, has begun to review new options to protect their assets and maintain the consumers' enjoyment of their products.

With the advent of mass consumer broadband access to the Internet, the requirement for an evolved form of copy protection has become paramount if owners of premium content are going to use this medium – DRM has been proposed and developed as a suitable solution. Some opponents cite DRM technologies as threatening the rights or privacy of the individual consumer. It should be noted that without a highly secure, flexible and easy-to-use system to protect, distribute and receive high-value content via the Internet, content owners such as major movie studios are unlikely to authorise the transmission of their premium content, thereby severely limiting premium content availability, retarding growth in this market and limiting the associated revenue opportunities.

The problem lies in the sheer complexity and variety of digital content products and their routes to consumers. Any solution must be scalable and flexible and enable secure distribution from end to end. It is also practical to expect that no single application can be applied for all users; what is required is a strategic complement of tools – a system – to protect digital content delivery.

For the software industry, where secure Internet deployment, registration and payment offer significant revenues today, a DRM solution has to be flexible and robust. The DRM requirements for software do not vary greatly from those described above for rich media over IP, but there are clear commercial advantages that can be achieved today:

- secure delivery of software by electronic download, on CD-ROM or DVD-ROM, or as value-added content on a video DVD;
- acceptance of payments and unlocking of products via the Internet and/or by phone, fax or e-mail; offering products on a time-limited trial basis (with or without 'click here to buy'), or on a subscription or rental basis;
- requiring users to activate or register their software;
- DRM protected software can only be used as intended.

A software company can therefore create an incremental revenue stream or transform their distribution and sales policies into a whole new way of doing business. SafeCast from Macrovision is an exceptionally flexible and highly secure DRM system; it supports the DRM 'wish list' quoted above and allows publishers to deliver software products via any digital medium and still retain complete control over how and when they can be 'unlocked' and used.

It is arguable that the market with the current greatest need of effective DRM is the audio marketplace, wherein over 20 years of producing audio CDs has led to the most significant widespread abuse of content owners' rights. Consumers may have the right in some countries to make a back-up copy of their CDs, but wholesale copying of top music labels' music has caused massive losses within the industry.

One main issue for the consumer lies in the dual nature of audio CD-ROM playback. When a copy-protected CD will work in a music system's CD tray, but will not work when placed in a PC, consumers may feel that their use is being compromised by copy protection and that they are being penalised. In November 2002, Midbar, an Israeli company with a commercially successful audio CD copy-protection product called Cactus Shield, was purchased by Macrovision to help produce a DRM solution by combining it with Macrovision's SafeAuthenticate product. A 'best of breed' solution is planned that would satisfy the rights concerns of the music industry and, at the same time, enable users to play their CDs in their PC, make compilation CDs, rip music to MP3 and enhance their listening range of options.

DRM is not about limiting access or simple copy protection. It has the means to be an enabling technology, transparent to legitimate consumers, which can also offer a wider choice of digital content and consumption within a secure framework.

One must also not forget that laws introduced in the 'analogue age' are highly unlikely to be effective in the more technologically advanced 'digital age'. To that end, and to be truly effective, legislation needs to take into account the fast changing nature of the digital world and protect not only the content but also the copy management technologies themselves against circumvention devices and means. It is to be hoped that the Government will clearly address this issue in the new Copyright Bill.

Macrovision Corporation (Nasdaq: MVSN) develops and markets electronic licence management digital rights management (DRM) and copy protection technologies for the enterprise software, consumer software, home video and music markets. Macrovision is headquartered in Santa Clara, California, with international headquarters in London and Tokyo.

Macrovision has copy protected over 3.5 billion VHS video cassettes and, in the last four years, one billion DVDs. Its copy protection technology is embedded in over 50 million digital set-top boxes including over 98 per cent of those used in the UK. These statistics and the company's extensive user base, which includes the Hollywood studios, the UK satellite and cable television industry, and the major PC games publishers, make Macrovision the world's leading copy protection provider for video, PC games and PPV television. Macrovision is now repositioning itself more as a rights management solution company and has developed and acquired patented technologies that provide DRM solutions for rich media (video/audio) delivered via IP (Internet), software and audio CD/DVDs.

Macrovision has developed a complete end-to-end DRM solution to support the distribution of rich media over a variety of distribution channels, including internet protocols (IP). This solution is called MacroSAFE. It is a multi-layered solution that enables video and audio content owners, software vendors and service providers to securely distribute their content to consumers and businesses – to enable them to maximise their revenue opportunities through new and cost-effective distribution channels. MacroSAFE is an enabling technology; users can get access to quality media and publishers have access to a wide range of business models – purchase, rental, subscription, time-restricted playback, number-restricted playback, pay-per-view, video-on-demand, and trial, free, and super distribution.

For further information contact: Macrovision UK Ltd, Charlwood House, The Runway, South Ruislip, HA4 6SE. Tel: +44 (0)20 88390400; Fax: +44 (0)20 8839 0409; Website: www.macrovision.com

Electronic licensing

Electronic licensing was originally developed to deter piracy, but is being adapted to improve software accountability, argues Simon Mehlman of Macrovision.

Electronic licensing is a great example of fulfilling big business demands by using simple, scalable systems; it cuts across a broad range of vertical markets, from chip developers to car manufacturers, from petrochemical companies to games developers. In essence, electronic licensing creates and enforces a simple business ethic: you get what you pay for.

Electronic licensing has its roots in the counter-offensive against software piracy. It has, however, evolved into a dynamic means for closing the gap between what software customers purchase and what they deploy. It has become a means to provide accountability to both software developers and software users, both stand-alone and networked.

Business users of software face a wide range of potential dangers in their use of software. Companies are liable for the actions of their employees, from sending unsuitable emails through to using illegal copies of software (such as ten people using an application for which the company only purchased a licence for five).

The Business Software Alliance (BSA) is one of the world's leading organisations dedicated to promoting a safe and legal online world. Whilst the BSA educates computer users on software copyrights and cyber-security, they are also very actively involved in the fight against software piracy in all its forms. In June 2002, in their seventh annual survey on software piracy, the BSA announced that:

> The rate of software piracy in the UK has dropped by one per cent to 25 per cent, the same level as in the United States ... Globally, however, software piracy is on the increase for the second year running, growing from 37 per cent in 2000 to 40 per cent in 2001. Global losses reached almost US$11 billion. Piracy rates in

Western Europe also increased three per cent on last year and currently stand at 37 per cent, equating to revenue losses of US$2.7 billion (almost 2.9 billion euros) for the software industry.

To support the fight against piracy the BSA will anonymously award up to £10,000 for every confidential report they receive that results in a successful prosecution.

Software piracy also impacts upon the revenues of both software users and developers. Users who 'under-license' their software requirements may experience constrictions in their workflow throughput. However, by over-licensing above their requirements – to be 'on the safe side' – companies can waste significant sums of money that could be better spent elsewhere.

It is the lack of accountability and the absence of a means to ensure and ultimately enforce licence compliance that threatened the revenues and continued development and growth of many in the software industry towards the end of the late 1980s. However, as economic pressures increased and as the growth in the adoption of software by industry was matched by an increase in the cost and value of software, particularly for networked software users, a means was required to enable developers to embed a simple system to ensure licence compliance in a user-friendly manner that could at the same time allow companies to enforce software licence compliance amongst their employees.

An early, and still popular, method is the use of a hardware key or 'dongle'. Dongles actually date back a lot further than people may imagine; one of their first commercial applications was in the field of 19th-century transport safety. A railway dongle was a large iron key that was used to unlock the points at either end of a stretch of single-track railway. This allowed exclusive use of the track by the train carrying the dongle.

Computer dongles now come in a variety of forms and usually connect to PCs via USB, parallel or serial communications ports. They are more commonly associated with access control rather than licence compliance; however, they can be integrated into an electronic licensing solution by assigning them a unique network ID code. Dongles provide a physical representation of security; however, they can break, they are subject to the same delays in supply and distribution that affect any hardware devices, and they can be lost or stolen, preventing businesses from accessing their software legitimately. Electronic licensing does not now require the presence of dongles, although some manufacturers still prefer to include them in their solution.

An example of electronic licensing for stand-alone applications is SafeCast by Macrovision (www.macrovision.com). SafeCast is an exceptionally flexible and highly secure digital rights management system for software. With SafeCast protection in place, developers and vendors can deliver software products securely via any digital medium, and still retain complete control over how and when they can be 'unlocked' (via an electronic licence) and used. SafeCast can accept payments and unlock products via the Internet and/or by phone, fax or email; it can even offer products as time-limited trials (with or without 'click here to buy' options) or on a subscription or rental basis and require users to register their product as part of the product activation.

Whilst this system of electronic licensing is suitable for stand-alone applications, it would be impractical for commercial software use by multiple users in a business network environment as it lacks true network accountability.

Metcalfe's Law states that: 'the value of a network grows by the square of the size of the network.' A network that is twice as large will be four times as valuable because there are four times as many things that can be done, due to the increased number of connections between nodes. An electronic licensing solution for network usage must be scalable, easy to embed and test by developers, easy to install by customers and easy to manage by system administrators – essentially it should be 'user-friendly'.

To provide a user-friendly licence enforcing system may at first appear to be something of a paradox. It is important to remember that any mechanism designed to ensure that users comply with licence terms, which can also supply authenticated usage data, must ensure that it is genuinely easy to use. When this is achieved, then a solution can be provided to overcome the shortcomings and financial penalties associated with licence abuse, and a whole new realm of possibilities arises for business software users and software developers.

To determine the importance of electronic licensing in our use of software, according to recent IDC data, in 2002 about 69 per cent of worldwide software sales – worth US$184 billion – used licences as opposed to 'shrink-wrapped' software. Out of all licences in 2002, about 70 per cent used electronic licences, representing US$89 billion in software value.

By 2006, IDC projects that 80 per cent of software will use licences, and 80 per cent of the licences, or software valued at US$185B (about twice current levels) will be distributed electronically.

Faced with these compelling arguments, the first decision faced by developers looking to incorporate electronic licensing is to determine whether they will generate this solution using internal resources. This can detract from core expertise and prove costly in terms of labour and reliance upon staffing shifts. By using a stable third-party supplier, developers can utilise existing expertise and retain their focus on their core product.

Software asset management audit tools for networked software applications can be used to analyse log files and provides companies using networked software a true measure of cost and usage accountability. Usage data enables accountability by allowing companies to analyse where software costs should be allocated, based on who used what and for how long. Peak and sustained demand can also be analysed and licence requirements adjusted accordingly in partnership with the vendor.

Through its evolution as a commercial technology, electronic licensing no longer simply offers business a means to limit the number of users of an application; it can be used to support access to a range of add-on feature sets and modules; it can enable timed trials and subscription-based pricing schedules. Electronic licensing can also be used to support 'pay-as-you-go' software use, by setting pricing policies in line with the data recorded within the network log file.

By using electronic licensing at the source code level, manufacturers are not only able to help companies enforce their licence agreements, they are able to help build new business models and pricing policies by adopting not just a single electronic licensing policy but, rather, a whole raft of flexible policies that can be easily adapted to the different requirements of varying customers, without the considerable expense of software rebuilds. The implications for a software developer range from minimal to far reaching – from minimising their licensing overheads through to a far greater impact upon the manner in which a company operates and generates its revenues.

Macrovision Corporation develops and markets electronic licence management, digital rights management (DRM) and copy protection technologies for the enterprise software, consumer software, home video and music markets. Macrovision is headquartered in Santa Clara, California, with international headquarters in London and Tokyo.

The Consumer Software Division provides an integrated suite of tools, such as SafeDisc and SafeCast, that enable developers and publishers to protect, distribute and promote their products securely and effectively, with built-in support for a wide range of robust business models.

The Globetrotter Enterprise Software Division's electronic licence management (ELM) solutions for business software applications, based upon the FLEXlm licensing toolkit, have been licensed to over 2,500 ISVs (independent software vendors) and Global 2000 enterprises worldwide over the last 13 years on over 40 platforms. FLEXlm allows a vendor to set conditions of access within a licence file that sits on a network server; to alter the licence terms, a new licence file can be generated, deployed (via the Internet) and installed at the customer's site by the network manager. Access to licensed applications is conditional upon licence file terms, and usage data is compiled within a log file, which can be analysed to assess usage data.

For further information contact: Macrovision, Globetrotter Enterprise Software Division, Vision House, Priory Court, Wellfield Road, Preston Brook, Cheshire, WA7 3FR. Tel: +44 (0)870 873 6300; Fax: +44 (0)1928 706 329; Website: www.globetrotter.com *or* Macrovision, Consumer Software Division, Charlwood House, The Runway, South Ruislip, HA4 6SE. Tel: +44 (0)20 8839 0400; Fax: +44 (0) 20 8839 0409; Website: www.macrovision.com

Security policies

Countering cybercrime

Improving risk management is imperative to countering cybercrime, according to the Fraud Advisory Panel, Cybercrime Working Group of the ICAEW.

In the past, companies have failed to deal with cybercrime, either due to lack of awareness or because of the stigma associated with being seen as a victim of fraud or another cyber-crime of this nature. There have also been few requirements that companies do take proactive steps to prevent this type of fraud. This approach is no longer acceptable and businesses must now act to ensure that they are adequately protected from, and prepared to take action in respect of, cybercrime. Taking adequate steps to improve an organisation's risk management in this area is no longer simply desirable, it is imperative.

Turnbull Guidelines

Whilst the provisions of the Turnbull Guidelines are only requirements for publicly listed companies, they are increasingly being viewed as the benchmark on good corporate governance for all companies listed in the UK and as the standard by which they may be judged.

Provision D.2 of the Turnbull Guidelines states that: 'The board should maintain a sound system of internal control to safeguard shareholders' investment and the company's assets.'

Provision D.2.1 states that: 'The directors should, at least annually, conduct a review of the effectiveness of the group's system of internal control and should report to all share-holders that they have done so. The review should cover all controls including financial, operational and compliance controls and risk management.'

Provision D.2.2 states that: 'Companies which do not have an internal audit function should periodically review the need for one.'

Data protection

Anyone who stores information about another person, be it for a commercial or other purpose, has a duty to maintain that data in accordance with the principles of data protection. This means that, as well as the requirement that the data stored is accurate and not stored for a period of time longer than necessary, the data must be kept secure.

This will require businesses to take steps to ensure that their computer systems and operational functions comply. The DTI provides a business standard benchmark called BS 7799 (now adopted as ISO 17799) for businesses and organisations attempting to comply with the Data Protection Act (1998) and other IT security issues. This is a common sense security standard that every business should benchmark themselves against (even if they do not go for full accreditation).

Human rights

The rights to privacy and family life are enshrined under the Human Rights Act 1998. Whenever a company or organisation stores information it must do so with these principles in mind, and it must take adequate steps to ensure that the organisation implements the correct controls and processes to ensure that the data is kept as secure as possible, so that in the event a company does suffer a cybercrime attack, the Human Rights principles are infringed to the least extent possible.

Liability of directors

Directors may, under the Turnbull Guidelines, find themselves in breach of duty to the company and, consequently, the shareholders for failing to carry out the correct risk management procedures and controls in respect of cybercrime.

Directors owe the company a number of fiduciary duties due to the position they hold within the company, including a duty of good faith and a duty to act with due diligence. They also owe duties of professional competence depending upon the terms of their service contract. If a director breaches the duties owed to the company he/she may face personal liability as against the company.

In the event that a company loses a substantial amount of money to a cyber-criminal it may not be possible, or not commercially viable, for that company to pursue the fraudster.

In that case a company may be obliged to look to the director responsible for the implementation of risk management for redress. If the director has failed to act with due care in respect of a foreseeable risk, this may result in the company seeking to establish that the director was liable for breach of a duty of care and to recover damages from that director.

Liability of accessories

It is important to appreciate that the person who has committed the fraud may not be the only person against whom a remedy can be obtained. There may be other people involved in committing the crime and therefore equally accountable.

For example, in the case of cyber-laundering, a firm may become liable by virtue of the principle of constructive trusteeship depending on whether they were at any point in receipt of laundered funds.

It is as a result of the principle of liability of accessories that banks and others used as a conduit by money launderers may find themselves in the difficult situation of trying to avoid becoming secondary victims.

Many countries and, notably, the European Union (EU) are looking to the registration authorities to verify the identity of e-traders by issuing digital certificates. There therefore may be scope for a claim against a particular registration authority (RA) that issues a certificate to a launderer.

Lawyers and accountants who have been involved in setting up any scheme may also be legitimate compensation targets.

Therefore, depending on the particular nature of your business, there are a multitude of different ways in which a business can incur liability for the cybercrimes of a fraudster.

The key to avoiding liability for money laundering is to 'know your customer'. Firms should take action in support of anti-money laundering measures in order to:

■ comply with legal requirements;
■ protect their corporate reputation.

Evidence of identity and beneficial ownership should be sought, and a higher level of due diligence undertaken, where there are:

■ numbered or alternative accounts;
■ high-risk countries involved;
■ offshore jurisdictions;
■ high-risk activities;
■ public officials involved.

Reviewing policy and procedure

Many firms will carry out financial controls, audits and assessments. The Turnbull Report places greater emphasis on the need for assessment of risk and operational controls. This means that senior management are required to review the procedures applied to risk management and control on an annual basis and decide which areas are lacking in such controls. Essentially they will have to start carrying out an internal audit of operational risk. The business benefit of this is that it can be stated on your annual accounts and could lead to greater trust by your customers and therefore increased business or market share.

In order to effectively review policy and procedure in terms of operational risk management, companies should be reviewing their Internet strategy and the related risk management issues at board level. In particular it is advisable that companies and organisations appoint one director to oversee the area where business strategy warrants this level of supervision, attaching responsibility for operational risk in relation to cybercrime to this individual or their department. This has the advantage of reducing the risk of criminal and civil prosecution of directors or the company for failure to comply with current standards and regulations, and it may well reduce long-term fraud losses. It may also reduce the chance that the company is rendered liable for receiving laundered or fraudulently obtained funds under the doctrine of constructive liability. However, the fight against cybercrime must be fought on all company levels. It is necessary to establish policy and procedure that apply to everybody in the business.

Cybercrime policy statement

A policy statement and settled working practices should be published by the board to ensure that every employee knows the standard required of them and the company stance in relation to cybercrime. Such a statement needs to be explained to every employee and should, ideally, be included in contracts of employment and supply and in outsourcing agreements.

The policy statement should be clear about the action that the company will take in the event that an act of cybercrime is detected. The statement should clearly express the company's policy towards cybercrime and its determination to deter fraud generally.

It should be made clear that the company:

■ will investigate and report to their local police or other appropriate authority any suspected acts of cybercrime;
■ will assist the police in their investigations and prosecution of a cyber-criminal if appropriate;
■ will take civil action where possible and recover assets that have been stolen, or pursue a cyber-criminal for damages;
■ expects employees to report any incidence of cybercrime of which they are aware, and assumes that each employee, irrespective of their level of seniority, has a responsibility for reporting cybercrime;
■ will treat internally perpetrated cybercrime as seriously as cybercrime perpetrated by an outsider;
■ has particular procedures that should be followed in the event that a cybercrime occurs.

The DTI report[1] says the increase in cybercrime is partly because companies give employees access to the Internet and their own work email addresses. It may also be of merit to include guidelines and company policy statements in relation to employee Internet and email use in their employment contracts. Example of such guidelines include highlighting the danger of opening emails with attachments from unknown sources, or listing sites that are prohibited from use, or explaining company policy in relation to Internet and software piracy (another common form of cybercrime).

Managing the prevention, detection and response to cybercrime

Cybercrime management should be dealt with throughout the organisation and the importance of employee awareness should be emphasised at all levels.

---

[1] Information Security Breaches Survey, DTI, April 2002.

Cybercrime needs to be treated as a business risk and an organisation therefore needs to carry out a risk management assessment procedure to ensure that the steps taken to prevent cybercrime are effective in relation to the practices peculiar to that organisation. Anti-cybercrime procedures should be tailored to match the type of business in which an organisation is involved. For example, an e-tailer is more likely to be concerned with establishing the identity of the individual attempting to carry out a 'card-not-present' transaction to make an online purchase as this type of business is more prone to the risk of identity theft and credit card fraud. In this case the fraudster is more likely to be an outsider. A business-to-business company that trades online may be more concerned with establishing procedures and controls that reduce the risk of e-procurement fraud and may wish to employ fraud detection methods such as data-mining or require procedures for the making of e-tenders. In the case of e-procurement fraud the fraud is far more likely to be perpetrated by an insider and the methods of detecting the fraud need to reflect this fact.

Risk management of the threat of cybercrime should be approached as follows. The company should:

■ identify the areas within the business that are most vulnerable to cyber-attack;
■ establish the controls that they already have in place to address these risks;
■ identify any further controls that may assist in reducing the risk;
■ monitor pre-existing controls to ensure that they are being implemented effectively;
■ assess the controls to account for any changes or developments made in the operation of the organisation;
■ ensure that procedures and controls are workable and supported by a sufficient level of resources;
■ establish a regular review procedure.

Whistle-blowing policy

All organisations should establish a culture of cybercrime awareness, and part of doing so is to ensure that employees know that whistle-blowing is a necessary part of the fight to prevent cybercrime.

Employees should have available to them a simple procedure for reporting any suspicion that cybercrime is taking place. This may include an internal email address to send details to, or a hotline to enable them to report their complaint quickly and, if the employee wishes to do so, anonymously.

It should also be made possible for the employee to report to management in different departments or management with no direct responsibility for that employee, given that the employee may fear that their direct manager is somehow implicated in an act of cyber-fraud.

It should be made clear to employees that all reports will be treated as confidential. Where such reports are made in good faith, the employee would normally be protected under the Public Interest Disclosure Act (PIDA) 1998.

This is particularly relevant to incidences of cybercrime where, as discussed earlier, a good proportion of the problem arises from the unlawful conduct of insiders and employees. The objective of the PIDA is to ensure that employees can inform their employers of wrongdoing within a company without fear of repercussions, allowing problems to be identified and resolved in as little time as possible. The repercussions referred to cover different types of detriment that an employee may suffer having made such a disclosure, including denial of a promotion or training opportunities, or of facilities that the employee would have been offered had it not been for the disclosure.

The employee is protected by PIDA if he makes a qualifying disclosure of information that he reasonably believes (and the employee can show that he reasonably believes) tends to show that one of the following offences or breaches have, are being or will be committed, irrespective of whether the employee is later shown to have been incorrect:

- a criminal offence;
- a breach of a legal obligation;
- a danger to the health and safety of any person;
- environmental damage;
- intentional concealing of information that demonstrates that any of the above have occurred.

The disclosure is protected if the employee makes the qualifying disclosure to his employer either by company procedures authorised by the employer or directly to the employer, or by making the disclosure to another person whom the worker reasonably believes to be solely or mainly responsible for the relevant failure.

The employee must also make the disclosure in good faith. If the employee wishes to make the disclosure to a prescribed body or person then he is protected if he makes the qualifying disclosure in good faith, he reasonably believes that any allegation or information is substantially true and reasonably believes that the matter falls within the remit of the prescribed person or body. For example if the information relates to a fraud the employee might reasonably think that the Serious Fraud Office would be the correct body to make the report to, or in the case of an offence relating to the environment, that the Environment Agency was the correct body.

Where a company does not have the resources to set up a whistle-blowing mechanism internally, it is possible to outsource this service. For serious cases of cyber fraud, it is possible to report the offence to the National Hi-Tech Crime Unit.

What to do when cybercrime is detected

It is necessary to maintain a procedure for dealing with any report of cyber-fraud. The procedure to be implemented will vary depending on the size of the business and the scale and seriousness of the cybercrime being investigated.

A firm may wish to appoint one person as responsible for investigating the cybercrime. They will in turn be responsible for researching the best methods of investigating a specific type of cybercrime.

This individual may also be given responsibility for assessing the in-house skills available for investigating cybercrime. For example whether the firm has anyone with the computer science skills to enable electronic evidence to be detected and preserved. It will also be necessary for that person to establish contacts with specialist lawyers and investigators.

Damage mitigation is another issue that must be addressed by the firm. It should be decided how it is possible to stop a particular cybercrime from happening again, and whether improved techniques of risk management are necessary.

It must be considered how the firm intends to secure and gather the evidence without alerting the criminal. The firm must address the question of how it intends to deal with a suspect and when it should contact the relevant authorities such as the National Hi-Tech Crime Unit.

As with all frauds, it must be considered when it is appropriate to inform the public that a cybercrime has occurred, bearing in mind the damage that such an announcement can have on a business compared to the value of the crime itself.

If an organisation does intend to prosecute a cybercrime it must bear in mind the following:

- speed;
- strategy;
- surprise.

Money is transferable by one email, telephone call or fax. It is therefore vital that not only is any investigation or analysis conducted in utmost secrecy but that action is taken before the fraudster has an inkling that he is being investigated.

At the very earliest opportunity an analysis should be carried out to assess:

- whether there has been any fraud;
- the extent of the fraud;
- whether it is viable to try and recover the losses sustained.

To do this it may be necessary to examine computer server logs and individuals' computers. Consult the list of 'Dos and Don'ts' at the end this chapter before taking any action, otherwise vital evidence needed for civil recovery or criminal action may be destroyed.

Third party disclosure as to assets and whereabouts

The English Courts provide invaluable assistance to victims of fraud in that, in certain circumstances, they grant orders that enable the victim, without notice to the fraudster, to discover:

- the extent of the fraud;
- who is responsible; and
- who was involved in the commission of the fraud and therefore could be liable as well.

The Court would, for example, grant orders against third parties who have been unwittingly involved in the fraud, whether such fraud has been committed electronically or in the physical world. For instance, the court will require disclosure of relevant information by an internet service provider or a bank through whom money stolen from the victim has passed.

Such orders for disclosure can be combined with what is called a 'gagging order', which prevents the party giving disclosure from notifying the fraudster. Breach of such an order will amount to a contempt of Court, which is punishable by prison.

Once the extent of the fraud has been assessed, decisions need to be taken as to whether it is commercially sensible (and whether there is an obligation) to pursue the fraudster and, if so, to what extent. No victim, however large or small, should fail to assess the significance of publicity, given the fact that it has been the victim of fraud, which is often caused by inadequate security measures or lack of judgement.

Recruitment, training and personnel policies

The majority of financial crime is perpetrated by insiders and employees. Cybercrime is no different. It is therefore essential for organisations to take appropriate steps to ensure that their computer and physical security is adequate. Personnel should be carefully vetted. References should be checked, and this includes temporary and contract staff. The procedure for vetting and checking should become more stringent when employees are promoted to greater positions of responsibility, and the greater the amount of personal, financial or sensitive data to which the employee is privy.

Employers should consider multi-level security, including biometric fingerprinting of employees and implementing similar security procedures of this nature to ensure that employees are only permitted access at an appropriate level to their role or seniority. Access levels should be reviewed on a frequent basis.

Employees who leave a firm (for any reason) should immediately be removed from the security clearance lists and any access to an organisation's database should be removed. Security lists should regularly be reviewed to ensure that those who do have access should have access, and whether access is necessary to the level that is permitted.

Employers should consider monitoring emails and communications in order to prevent fraud and other forms of cybercrime where it is warranted, but they should inform employees in general that this is likely to occur.

Collaboration with government agencies and professional advisory bodies

Organisations should consider collaborating with governmental and professional advisory organisations to report how they manage information security and cybercrime threats, and work with suppliers and users to co-ordinate information on incidents. This will assist businesses in plugging the knowledge and information gaps, assessing where risk management procedures are lacking and where a business's vulnerabilities lie.

In connection with this, organisations may find it of great assistance to collaborate with government and industry advisory bodies to produce educational materials on the nature of cybercrime, why it has posed a problem for their particular business and how they have obtained information and guidance on the subject.

Ultimately, reviewing existing guidance and producing further guidance on basic information security requirements and good risk management practice to combat cybercrime could be used to produce a 'superhighway code'. This would ideally take into account BS 7799, organisations established by the Information Systems Audit and Information Control Association and also the work of the IT Governance Institute in the United States.

The aim is to eventually raise general awareness among industry, accountancy and the legal professions of the law relating to cybercrime and its effective precaution.

Compliance

No procedure or control is effective unless properly implemented throughout an organisation. Regular checks must be undertaken in order to ensure that all necessary controls are being adequately implemented by employees at all levels, short cuts are not used in such a way as to dilute the effectiveness of controls, and that the controls remain effective in the light of changes in the law or in the development of the organisation's business.

Dos and don'ts for computer based information

Computer evidence or data is fundamentally different from, say, paper evidence. Just the act of turning on a computer can change a whole series of dates and times and invalidate its use in a court or tribunal. Therefore, a few basic principles need to be followed when dealing with potentially valuable computer evidence.

Do:
■ fully assess the situation before taking any action;
■ isolate the computer so that it cannot be tampered with;
■ record where the computer is based and all who had access to it;
■ consider securing all relevant logs (eg building access logs, server logs, Internet logs) and any CCTV footage at the earliest opportunity;
■ call in IT security staff or external consultants as appropriate.

Then ask the relevant expert to:

■ disconnect the relevant computers from your network;
■ restrict remote access;
■ take an 'image' copy of the computer.

Don't:
■ alert any of the potential suspects;
■ call in your own IT support staff (they often change evidence inadvertently);
■ turn on the computer if it is switched off;
■ turn off the computer if it is turned on;
■ move the computer if it is switched on;
■ make a copy of the computer;
■ examine electronic logs without first ensuring that they are preserved elsewhere.

The Institute of Chartered Accountants in England and Wales (ICAEW) is the largest professional accountancy body in Europe, with over 122,000 members. For more information on its Fraud Advisory Panel email info@fraudadvisorypanel.org.

Security as standard

By emphasising management systems, the British Standards Institute is hoping to help companies improve their security from the inside out.

'Walls have ears' – this slightly surreal cautionary wartime note was one of the first warnings about confidentiality that most of the British public had ever heard. But it presaged an imperative that was soon accepted by almost every organisation in every country in the world – the need for caution, thoroughness and foresight in avoiding the leak of business-critical information to enemies or competitors.

In three decades the battlefront has moved from the waste bin and the pub to IT, telemetry and corporate governance.

Of course, the stakes are now so high that information security has spawned a whole industry – and a rewarding one. But different organisations have approached it in different ways. Perhaps because matters of confidentiality and security are discussed only 'on a need to know basis'. Perhaps because the technology of espionage and counter-espionage is so precious it's kept close to the chest. And perhaps because bosses and IT managers don't like to deal with outside authorities on matters so intimate.

Varying standards of security equipment are permissible. You get what you pay for – and anyway there are British standards (BS) and international standards (ISO) to cover product and service quality aren't there?

But what about best practice in the organisations that wish to be protected? How do they know they're following the right approach? Equally important, how can their suppliers and customers be reassured that their own confidential information and trading secrets are not being misused?

Establishing the standards

Towards the end of the last millennium the British Standards Institute knuckled down to establishing an information security standard. Following extensive consultation with industries and organisations all over the world, they developed BS 7799 Part 1 Information Security Management – Code of practice for information security management and BS 7799 Part 2 Information Security Management – Specification for information security management systems.

BS 7799 promoted protection for intellectual property, in the same way that material goods have traditionally been protected. It reminded us of how important a business reputation can be to customer confidence and, ultimately, to profits. Amongst its benefits, the promotional material listed 'fewer crises' and 'less risk of litigation'.

An Audit Commission survey of 900 UK organisations revealed that half of the public sector organisations interviewed and a third of private sector companies had been affected by IT fraud or abuse.

The professional world was quickly coming to the conclusion that a simple lapse in information security can damage an organisation's credibility, reduce customer confidence and, ultimately, damage profits.

The whole point of establishing standards is to promote the widespread standardisation of working practice; so it was inevitable that such a significant business issue was recognised to be a universal problem – one demanding a worldwide standard. Thus, it was only a matter of time before the British standard BS 7799 Part 1:1999, became the internationally recognised ISO standard ISO/IEC 17799:2000, Code of Practice for Information Security.

In the few years between the development of the original BS 7799 and the ISO/IEC 17799 standards, there had been a sea change in BSI's philosophy: the institution recognised that standards alone could be viewed as prescriptive and restrictive – that is, if you hadn't got the working practices in place to meet the relevant criteria, the standard would be perceived as little more than a set of rules.

The new enlightened view was that what businesses need is management systems – in short, the structure, philosophy and working methods that inherently meet the values defined by the standard. This led to the development and release of BS 7799–2:1999 and subsequently to the release of the revised standard BS 7799 Part 2:2002 – Information Security Management Systems: Specification with Guidance for Use. Part 2 of BS 7799 then becomes a basis for the organisation's own information security management system (ISMS).

By emphasising management systems, BSI was more able to help organisations to improve their efficiency from the inside out, whereas an emphasis on standards meant change from the outside in. BS 7799–2:2002 introduces a better way of working, based on a management system that, with its in-built facility for constant improvement, is self-perpetuating.

Nowhere was there a greater need for consistent, focused working patterns and management practices than in the field of information security. It is a field in which care and attention have to permeate throughout the organisation – from the CEO to the casual cleaner. This was a management system that could not afford to be the concern solely of the quality manager or the CEO or the IT manager – it demanded commitment from everyone in the organisation.

Both the BS and ISO/IEC standards address the issues related to conventional paper-based information systems, analogue communications, digital communications and IT-based information systems. It is worth noting that the original BS standard was conceived during the hysteria of the 'dotcom bubble' – it was, rightly, perceived that speed and prevalence of email and other digital communication posed a phenomenal risk to information security. Data was travelling faster and further than ever before, and could be readily copied and compressed into ever-smaller media.

What the international standard covers

So what does the ISO/IEC 17799:2000 document address? It provides guidelines on how the various controls that are identified in BS 7799–2:2002 Annex A can be implemented by an organisation developing an Information Security Management System (ISMS). Although providing detailed information on these controls, it should be remembered that the end-user is advised to use the controls as appropriate to their business, and to identify and implement other controls that they may determine to be more suitable to their business. However, wherever possible the ISO/IEC 17799:2000 document should be used in parallel with, and as a supporting document for, any registration or compliance statement to BS 7799–2:2002.

An ISMS, as defined in BS 7799–2:2002, must cover all of the following:

- management responsibility including management commitment, and resource management;
- management review of the ISMS including review input, review output and internal audits;
- ISMS improvements including continual improvements, corrective actions and preventative actions;
- a security policy – a document that demonstrates management support and commitment to the ISMS process;
- security organisation – a management framework to implement and sustain information security within your organisation;
- asset clarification and control – an inventory of assets, with responsibility assigned for maintaining security;
- personnel security – job descriptions for all staff, outlining their security roles and responsibilities;
- physical and environmental security – a definition of the security requirements for your premises and the people within them;
- communications and operations management – a method of ensuring that your communications operate within secure parameters;
- access control – network management to ensure that only authorised people have access to relevant information, and to protect the supporting infrastructure;
- systems development and maintenance – to ensure that IT projects and support activities are conducted securely, using data control and encryption where necessary;
- business continuity management – a managed process for protecting critical business processes from major disasters or failures;

■ compliance – evidence of your commitment to meet statutory or regulatory information security requirements, for your clients, employees and relevant authorities.

Most organisations will already have some of these in place, but few will be doing every-thing. BSI client managers are experienced in working with companies to evaluate their current system's merits, and in guiding them through the steps necessary to develop their management system to the point where it can be registered under the standard.

BSI have developed client service into a fine art – they can arrange training schemes to train clients' staff, they can provide written and digital training materials for self-study and they arrange regular seminars all over the country to introduce thought-provoking and informative angles on BS 7799–2:2002 and other management systems.

Through its intimate relationship with businesses all over the world, BSI has learned very graphically that standards – and, indeed, management systems – are not an end, but merely a means. But to what?

Benefits

The benefits are expressed as 'benefiting the bottom line' – that is, supporting the private sector objectives of efficiency and profitability – although, clearly, non-profit-making organisations stand to benefit in other no less valuable ways. When you consider the health, education and police services, it's obvious that BS 7799–2:2002 could be even more relevant to the public sector.

The direct and indirect benefits of operating a management system based on BS 7799–2:2002 include:

■ improved employee motivation;
■ increased efficiency;
■ better use of time and resources;
■ cost savings;
■ increased competitiveness;
■ increased customer satisfaction;
■ confidence throughout the supply chain;
■ fewer crises;
■ less risk of litigation;
■ wider market opportunities;
■ increased profits.

And there are further advantages. BSI point out that once an organisation's ISMS is regis-tered to BS 7799–2:2002, it's in a good position to integrate this system with a quality management or environmental management system, to create an integrated management system.

Conclusion

This chapter began with the slogan 'walls have ears'. It should end with the slightly more sinister message that 'knowledge is power'. Over the years, successive boardroom coups have demonstrated that information has a tangible value and a very powerful influence over the fortunes of organisations and individuals.

In today's broadband, satellite communication world, ISMSs shouldn't need much selling. The need for them is obvious – you cannot be unaware of how much information flows to and from your desktop, your department, your domain.

While the threats are often invisible, it's reassuring that the solution is tangible and accessible. BS 7799–2:2002 and its supporting document ISO/IEC 17799:2000 are logical, practical to implement and easy to sustain. Are you going to go for it? Mind who you tell, or it'll be all round the building…

BSI is a group of complementary businesses, all working to the same vision of support for business improvement and trade worldwide. We believe in the universal adoption of best management practices, reduction of risk throughout the trading process and the harmonisation and acceptance of standards by consent as a means of achieving economic prosperity. For further information contact: BSI Group, 389 Chiswick High Road, London W4 4AL. Tel: +44 (0)20 8996 7720; Website: www.bsi-global.com

Adequate security

Even a basic written policy on information security cuts out some of the main risks to a business, says Chris Knowles from Computacenter. It is surprising that so few companies have one.

Most UK companies recently surveyed spend approximately one per cent of their IT budget on security, well below the recommended spend on security of three per cent of IT budgets or 10 per cent of IT budgets in the case of financial services companies. Only 27 per cent of companies spend more than one per cent of IT budgets on security. It is important to remember that security spend needs to be justified in terms of business benefit and return on investment (ROI) with a comprehensive cost/risk-benefit analysis, especially as you need to be sure that any security spend can be fully explained to your board members.

So what technologies are companies currently spending their security pounds on? Research by industry analysts suggests that the most highly implemented network security elements are server and workstation security, network perimeter firewalls and remote access and authentication services. The aim for many enterprises is to secure the visible weaknesses in their environments and to develop new security architectures.

Where to start implementing IT security

Any enterprise wanting to make improvements in security must take a broad view of its information assets and understand their value as well as the threats to these assets and their vulnerabilities.

The first thing a company should then ascertain is whether or not there are any existing company security policy documents. This is a formal published document that defines roles, responsibilities, acceptable use and enterprise security practices. Very few companies have a formal written security policy in place; however, if there isn't one to refer to, how can you determine whether or not you've applied all the correct security measures? With even a basic security policy in place, organisations can go some way to alleviating some of the key risks to their business. For example, according to Gartner: '90 per cent of security breaches take advantage of poorly configured or unpatched servers; such breaches are easily preventable if security processes are followed.'

Companies with existing security policies generally have a far greater understanding and appreciation of why they need to manage the confidentiality, integrity and availability of their information assets, than those without such policies. Nevertheless, if you are considering implementing a security policy framework, Computacenter recommends that the policies are not created in isolation. As Gartner comments: 'Because a security policy affects all parts of an enterprise, it should be created by a collaborative process that involves participation from the IS department, human resources (HR) and legal, administrative and executive business teams.'

But adequate security isn't just about policies, especially if it's to be the business enabler that it should be. It's about making services, applications and information securely available at the right cost, to the right people, at the right time, and from the right place. Only by understanding how end-user services are delivered and by conducting a company-wide audit can you assess the risks and vulnerabilities they are subjected to. It is essential to look at the bigger picture; IT security extends beyond protecting against the actions of recently terminated employees to unknown threats and risks. As a result of carrying out such an audit, areas you need to prioritise, address and subsequently manage will become evident.

From the findings of their Security Breach Survey for 2002, the DTI has compiled a checklist to help companies who are looking to implement security solutions.

1. Staff education – create a security aware culture.
2. Have clear, up-to-date security policies in place.
3. Assign dedicated staff to security – as well as using external consultancy staff as needed – policing the policemen.
4. Evaluate security spend and the ROI on that spend.
5. Build security into all IT requirements rather than trying to bolt it on later.
6. Keep technical defences up-to-date – patched server operating systems, etc.
7. Put in place procedures to ensure compliance with regulatory requirements.
8. Have contingency plans to respond to a serious security breach or incident.
9. Understand the status of insurance coverage against damage from a breach.
10. Test the compliance with/of your security policy – audits, penetration tests etc.

Different approaches to security

Many data security issues are common sense – just as you wouldn't drive a car on the road without brakes, similarly you shouldn't put unprotected web servers on the Internet. The risks are simply too great. Adequate IT information security is about being able to reduce those risks by continually:

Protecting

This means sufficiently recognising, prioritising and protecting your organisation's information assets by acknowledging the wide abuses they could be subject to because of their importance, uses and location – this primarily involves business issues concerning people, policies and processes.

Detecting

You must be able to recognise abuses no matter who or what is responsible for them – this involves people, policies, technology, settings and processes.

Responding

You should defend your assets from misuse either automatically or with rapid decision-making, or even with manual intervention, to stop the misuse. The word 'continually' is key here. IT security is not about buying hardware and software, setting it up and then forgetting about it. New risks and vulnerabilities occur every day, especially as hackers get smart to new technologies and applications. Adequate security requires continual assessment and vigilance by your security team, excellent processes and thoroughly planned quality controlled updates.

Roadmaps and the 80:20 rule

IT security is very much governed by the same 80:20 rule, or Pareto Principle, used in marketing, except in this case, whilst 80 per cent of security is people, processes and documentation, only 20 per cent of security is the technology. There are quite a few standard security roadmaps and guidelines around. Below we provide you with a quick overview of these standards as a reference point for your further research:

■ BS 7799 and ISO 17799 are perhaps the most authoritative guidelines that make an organisation consider security in a holistic way and at least recognise the wide range of risks they face. BS 7799 also offers BS Certification. As the BS 7799 guidelines (rapidly becoming BS/ISO 17799) are not only the UK standard, but are now also accepted worldwide, these guidelines are essential reading and provide an excellent starting point for a holistic best-practice security framework. Organisations can be certified to the BS 7799 standard, which makes it an attractive condition to put in tenders. In particular, financial services companies are keen to work with BS 7799 compliant or accredited partners (see www.bsi-global.com).
■ The global Information Security Forum (ISF) through Citicus delivers Internet-based automation for implementing the ISF's FIRM (Fundamental Information Risk Management) methodology.
■ *Information Security Policies Made Easy* is an updated collection of over 1,100 security policies and templates covering virtually every aspect of corporate security. Written by Charles Cresson Wood, CISA, CISSP, it is an excellent all-in-one security policy resource with templates, advice and instructions to help you generate practical, clear and compelling information security policies for any organisation.

- There are also the many security organisations such as CERT and SANS Institute (www.sans.org) and the ICSA Labs run by TrueSecure (www.icsalabs.com), who provide 'best practice' information.
- In addition there are numerous other 'white papers' and guides available from security software vendors, research companies and the major consultancy firms, such as Symantec, ISS, Gartner, Meta Group and Forrester.

The 'Seven Rules' approach

A rather simplistic yet more pragmatic way of looking at IT security is the 'Seven Rules' approach to website security, which Computacenter has updated below so it can also apply to networks:

1. Have/create a security plan

Have a solid security plan and adequate policies in place – ideally before you open your new systems to real-world users and hackers! Also, ensure that you conduct regular vulnerability assessments and penetration tests on all your systems.

2. Understand your risk levels

Regular assessment lets you set the levels of risk you are taking and relate them to your 'adequate' security protection posture. It is important to remember that while security is an enabler, it also takes both time and money to implement, so systems should not be made substantially more complex for end-users. For instance, you may want a simple password system to allow users to access low-value information services but more complex authentication and authorisation procedures for more confidential, sensitive or valuable information. A leading IT portal, CW360.com, recommends using at least an eight-character password that doesn't relate to users' lives and isn't made up of dictionary words or dates. It suggests that, 'a password must be easy for the owner to remember, yet resist intuitive cracking'. And that's the problem, and why in real life they are usually so insecure!

3. Don't depend on firewalls

You need them, but there's more to a complete security system than just adding one to external connections to your local area network. Firewalls are often single points of failure, so work out the implications of losing connectivity or external access to systems. What's the risk or cost to your organisation? Don't forget to consider HA (high availability) solutions. A badly configured firewall is often more dangerous to an organisation than no firewall at all, so make sure that when you set up rules for usage, you have stringent testing procedures to reveal any potential loopholes and examine daily firewall logs correlated with your other network security log information. According to Vnunet.com, approximately nine per cent of firewalled networks suffer security breaches. Computacenter's recommendation is to be aware that, at heart, a firewall is a dumb protocol-rules and packet-inspection engine – a single defence layer that can be compromised – so even if it's set up correctly, you always need more protection layers!

4. Have an access policy

Have an access policy and ensure that it is adhered to. As is common in most environments, you will need different levels of user access. You want customers to buy goods online, but you do not want to provide hackers with an open door to your system and data. You also want to authenticate remote and teleworkers more stringently, as well as their system authorisations and privileges. Access via wired or wireless connections and devices needs to be examined to ensure that it is secure. Strong authentication and encrypted virtual private network (VPN) links are a good place to start.

5. Test, test, test

Get somebody else to test your security regularly. Ethical hackers and security service providers are now being employed by companies such as IBM to break into client networks and find their weak spots. Whilst it may be worrying to think that you are offering someone else the chance to break into your system, it is essential to independently test your systems and act upon the findings of those tests.

6. Keep monitoring

Monitor your security regularly, ideally using software-alerting and management tools, and ensure that results are analysed. This may sound obvious, but companies often don't check and review security procedures once they're in place, and regular monitoring can identify any changes that need to be made as your network and/or your website's functions and capabilities evolve.

7. Plan for disaster

Have plans in place for when it all goes wrong. This should be a natural progression from the vulnerability assessment, but it is often forgotten about. All organisations should have contingency plans, covering areas such as who should be contacted in the event of a breach, what back-up systems are required and/or disaster recovery provisions. Vnunet.com suggests that seven out of ten companies have no disaster recovery strategy in place and that a serious systems crash would put their companies in dire straits. Whilst these approaches may appear simplistic, they do communicate the basic need for you to start establishing some form of framework that works within and supports the maxim 'some security is better than no security'.

Conclusion

Security is clearly becoming a big issue for enterprises; however, not all companies have yet adopted sufficient security measures.

There is no great mystery behind information security, and there are a number of roadmaps out there to help you, no matter how basic or sophisticated your business, to prioritise and create an ROI for every layer of security you adopt.

The key message is that it's important to start considering the risks, build company-wide security policies and justify the deployment and management of security technology within all your new IT initiatives. User education is also imperative to the implementation of a successful IT security solution and should be built into any security solution. However, it must be recognised that security is not an end in itself: it enables businesses to protect themselves from major threats in their operating environments and to carry out processes and transactions that are otherwise too risky to carry out. Importantly, it is a continual process of assessment and evaluation. Businesses change, IT infrastructures change and, unfortunately, attackers get smarter.

Deploying the right security technologies is by no means an easy task. As George Anderson at Computacenter comments: 'Security is a key component that must cut across the infrastructure stack no matter what the layer. It's essential that organisations take a holistic approach – a single weakness can mean that the walls come crumbling down.'

The Computacenter Security Practice specialises in providing vendor-independent information security solutions, consultancy and services to the public and commercial sectors, often in the role of a trusted security advisor. As our customers have opened up their networks to embrace new and interactive technologies, and in response to the greatly increased risks that have made tight security business-critical, Computacenter has developed a breadth and depth of skills and expertise in the IT security services sector.

For further information contact: Computacenter (UK) Ltd, Hatfield Avenue, Hatfield, Hertfordshire AL10 9TW. Email: enquiries@computacenter.com; Website: www.computacenter.com

A multi-layered response

'Security in depth and security in breadth' is the key when putting together an information policy, says Paul Barker, Technical Architect at Integralis.

Many of the problems associated with information security arise from the tendency of most organisations to take a 'sticking plaster' approach to the issue, in that they identify that a threat exists or that a security incident has occurred and then determine a specific control in order to manage or mitigate the particular threat. The problem with this approach is that it is generally reactive and inconsistent, and it is simply not extensive enough as it does not consider other threats.

A lack of consistency can be a serious problem, as security incidents can take a variety of forms. In its broadest sense an incident can be anything from the loss, damage, theft or non-availability of information to the violation of internal policies. Furthermore, these risks can come from within or from outside the organisation, and they may be purely accidental or blatantly malicious.

In reality approximately 80 per cent of reported incidents come from within the organisation and are mostly the result of ignorance or carelessness. Only a small percentage are malicious and these tend to come from disgruntled employees, ex-employees or hackers. The major concern is that these malicious incidents tend to have a high cost in terms of lost revenue or company credibility – in some instances share prices of companies have tumbled. The obvious conclusion is that information security must address equally internal threats and external threats.

Incidents originating from outside the organisation are generally:

■ website defacement – this is where a page on the web server (typically the home page) is modified in order to announce to the world that the site has been hacked;
■ denial of service (DOS) – this is where a hacker will cause a system or application to crash (often repeatedly); this results in loss of revenue and, potentially, loss of customers.

Incidents originating from inside the organisation are generally:

■ web surfing of non-business-related sites resulting in loss of productivity (ie revenue);
■ service disruption resulting from unscheduled or untested changes to the environment;
■ illegal activity such as downloading pornographic material (such as paedophilia);
■ unwittingly introducing some form of virus into the environment, typically through email or file sharing;
■ attempted access to systems or information by unauthorised persons (either accidental or malicious);
■ leaving classified or sensitive information on screen, visible to unauthorised persons;
■ leaving systems logged in, unattended and accessible to passing persons;
■ wrongful disclosure of personal information (in contravention of the Data Protection Act 1988);
■ accidental deletion of information.

The most serious incidents are rare but can prove very costly, whether they are internally or externally inspired. Internal staff are better positioned to exploit situations as they are typically 'trusted', with a good understanding of the systems, applications and architecture. An external hacker needs to be highly skilled, using a combination of analysis skills, code creation and even social engineering (the manipulation of people to obtain information). These rare types of incidents include:

■ theft of information – such as customer details. These would typically be sold to, or taken to, competitive companies.
■ theft of information – such as credit card details. Once extracted these can be sold to the criminal world for fraudulent purposes.
■ theft of information – such as ideas, products or solutions (ie industrial espionage). This could provide a company with a competitive advantage.
■ embezzlement – this requires the perpetrator to understand how an organisation's business operates, specifically in terms of accounting and cash-flow, in order to divert funds (easier for internal staff).

People controls

When considering the controls to be used to address the security issue, we must consider where and how we can influence behaviour.

When considering the external threat, an organisation can exert very little influence over the behaviour of users entering its website, and as such are dependent on utilising technology products or product configurations in order to either make the environment (internet access, servers and applications) robust, or to detect, alert and potentially repel malicious activity.

When considering the internal threat, an organisation has far more influence over the behaviour of users utilising internal systems and information. Users must be made aware of what is acceptable behaviour and of the consequences of unacceptable behaviour. This can be achieved by utilising policies and training to educate users, to commit them through employment contracts and to engender security awareness as part of day-to-day activity.

Another cause of internal security breaches arises from modifications to applications, systems or infrastructure, without adequate consideration for testing, back-up and back-out where these cause down-time and cause the risk for security weaknesses to be brought into the internal infrastructure. This is adequately addressed within an effective change control process that has consideration for security impact.

Reporting and recovering from a security breach

In any instance that a security breach occurs, the training and education process should ensure that staff recognise an event and are aware of the process for reporting the event (who has responsibility), and that those persons with responsibility know the process for handling the event. These policies and procedures would entail such elements as:

■ procedures for handling staff who have contravened company security policies – such procedures should contain the ultimate threat of dismissal or prosecution;
■ procedures for detecting security breaches (tools, logs etc).
■ procedures for recovering from specific types of incident (rebuild of operating system, restore from back-up etc).
■ communication procedures – keeping users, customers and trading parties informed of the incident, its impact and the progress of recovery.
■ management procedures – identifying the forum to manage the incident process and consider damage limitation in the communication process.

Contractual controls

Another element to consider is the potential threat (either accidental or malicious) from third parties with whom there is some formal relationship (such as trading partners or service providers); these may in some instances be considered as trusted, however, the threat still exists.

With a trading partner a sensible approach is to make them responsible for their own actions, in addition to providing protective controls. A contract may state that they must demonstrate that 'reasonable and considered' controls are taken relative to the form of communication, sensitivity of the information and the potential threat. Contractual terms would then seek agreement on an interpretation of these controls and should also provide regular opportunities to have the controls demonstrated to the satisfaction of your organisation. At the point that the third party enters an organisation, controls should also be implemented.

With a service provider, a contract should not only consider those conditions that apply to a trading partner, but should also consider how loss of the service provided by them would impact the service offered to customers and trading partners. In this respect, the contract should agree service level commitments that can be effectively monitored and proven, and should agree compensation for failure to achieve the service levels.

Technology controls

Where technology controls are used, it is important that they are configured and maintained as effectively as possible. Some security controls will be inherent within the products being used, such as operating systems (account passwords, file permissions etc); others will require specialist security products such as perimeter controls (firewalls etc) and content controls (anti-virus or mobile code protection, intrusion detection systems (IDS) etc). There is little point in deploying such controls merely to achieve a 'tick in the box' to a 'top-level-down' exercise to implement security.

Many organisations will be dependent upon utilising a specialist security company in order to ensure effective security through technology controls. This will often encompass multi-layer security (security in depth) to exploit and combine:

- tight access controls;
- strong authentication;
- protection of information in transit (encryption);
- hardened operating systems, services and applications;
- high availability;
- quality of service;
- performance.

Acts of God or terrorism

In the event that an incident occurs that is considered exceptional, such as flooding, lightning, vehicle crash, bomb explosion or significant loss of key staff (to lottery win, for example), an organisation must have plans in place to minimise the impact to the business by restoring a level of service within a pre-determined time-frame and managing the communications process between staff, partners and customers (ie business continuity).

Insurance

When all reasonable measures have been taken, an organisation should also consider insurance. In the case of a significant security incident, insurance funds will limit the damage to the business by providing some element of (or all of) the revenue to recover the business to the point of normal operation.

This form of insurance is often referred to as cyber-liability insurance. Some insurance companies specialise in such policies, but will often require some evidence that adequate controls have been implemented before a policy can be obtained.

Maintaining effective security

A management process for information security (policy-based controls) needs to encompass a mechanism for review. This mechanism should consist of an audit process to regularly review the business operations, the risks and the controls in order to ensure the policy-based controls remain effective.

The technology controls also need to encompass a mechanism for review. This mechanism should consist of a regular audit of the complete technology infrastructure to review the technology operations, the risks and controls, and, importantly, to ensure that the technology controls remain effective. In addition, this review should encompass regular vulnerability and penetration testing.

In both cases the primary purpose is to refine the controls each time the review is performed, thus optimising the controls, or ensuring that the controls are the most appropriate through experience. The process also ensures that information security adapts with changes to the organisation and changes with the way business is performed.

The standards-based approach

Any organisation that undertakes an exercise to implement 'information security' using the management approach to achieve consistent, extensive and comprehensive security will normally need to look for guidance.

An own 'best efforts approach' has obvious limitations; it is far better to utilise an approach based upon best practice that has some form of track record – the obvious being an existing standard that specifically addresses the requirement. Several such standards exist that address the requirements to varying degrees.

The BS 7799 and ISO 17799 standards

The ISO 17799 standard started life as the British Standard BS 7799 Part 1 Code of Practice for Information Security in 1995. The creation of the standard was instigated by the Department of Trade and Industry (DTI) within the United Kingdom under instruction from the British Government. The DTI charged the British Standards Institute (BSI) with producing the standard; it was formed with input from leading British and international companies based upon best practices.

The code of practice (BS 7799 Part 1) provides guidance on what should be encompassed in, and the methodology for structuring, resources and processes to achieve information security. This was then accompanied by BS 7799 Part 2, this being a specification for an information security management system (ISMS).

In 2000 the BS 7799 Part 1 code of practice was submitted to the ISO committee for consideration as an international standard and was accepted and ratified later in 2000 as ISO 17799. The ISO 17799 standard has now superseded the BS 7799 Part 1 standard (which has been withdrawn). The BS 7799 Part 2 standard continues to apply and continues to provide a process for achieving certification.

The ISO 17799 standard defines information security as:

- confidentiality: ensuring that information is accessible only to those authorised to have access;
- integrity: safeguarding the accuracy and completeness of information and processing methods;
- availability: ensuring that authorised users have access to information and associated assets when required.

This top-level-down approach (management process) is more likely to succeed than many other approaches because it recognises the need for top-level commitment to ensure that the company has the desire and motivation to undertake such a project; and through top-level commitment come the resources and funding to achieve success. Without board-level buy-in, a successful implementation is very difficult to achieve.

The ISO 17799 standard focuses upon ten key areas:

- security policy – a board-level statement of commitment and approach to information security;
- security organisation – the structure of people, functions and responsibilities in relation to information security and the standard;
- asset classification and control – the identification of what should be protected and the importance placed on the various assets;
- personnel security – the vetting, contracts, acceptable behaviour and disciplinary procedures relating to employees, third parties and service providers;
- physical and environmental security – the physical locks, monitoring systems, access control systems, services and utilities required for the environment to be protected and to function;
- computer and network security – the infrastructure, third-party network and Internet controls, help desk and support services;
- system access controls – the password control, authentication, authorisation, systems-builds and privileges;
- systems development and maintenance – the code and version control, testing facilities and change control processes;
- business continuity planning – ensuring that a plan exists specifying what actions an organisation will take to recover business operation in the event of a major incident;
- compliance – this ensures that an organisation operates within the law in respect of applicable acts and laws, including copyright, piracy, data protection etc.

In very simple terms the ISO 17799 approach is to:

- determine the scope;
- create a 'people environment' to make the process work;
- identify what information needs to be protected based upon some form of priority;
- determine the policies, procedures and technical controls that currently exist;
- perform an audit of the information and environment;
- determine if the existing policies, procedures and controls are suitable or require enhancement;
- perform a risk analysis;
- select controls;

- implement controls;
- perform periodic audits to refine, update or replace the controls.

One of the significant points about the ISO 17799 approach is that any existing policies, procedures or controls that are currently used by an organisation are retained wherever possible. These may need to be enhanced before they are adequate and suitable, but only if they are totally unsuitable are they disregarded.

Neither the ISO 17799 standard nor the BS 7799 Part 2 standard are intended to specify the technology products to be implemented, or to specify how technology controls should be configured or tested to obtain the most effective security possible.

This is not a failing of the standard, but these limitations should be recognised. Organisations should NOT assume that, because controls have been implemented in accordance with the standard, the technology controls are effective.

Conclusion

This methodology is suitable for any organisation that aims to utilise a dual approach to the provision of information security that is extensive, consistent and effective – ie 'security in depth and security in breadth'. The management element based upon the ISO 17799 information security standard, and the use of audit, installation, project and testing services to provide the effective technology controls.

It is the process of integrating these two elements, such that the results of the technology services are reflected back within the ISO 17799 process, which creates a unique approach and an effective overall solution.

Integralis, the corporate solutions division of Articon-Integralis, provides information security solutions to all industry sectors throughout world, allowing organisations to grow and achieve their business goals securely. These solutions combine services and system integration, the deployment of 'best-of-breed' security products and managed security services, and employ some of the leading technologists and most skilled engineers in the industry. Integralis is recognised as a leading and trusted provider of Information Security Solutions in the European IT and e-commerce security market.

For further information contact: Integralis Ltd, Theale House, Brunel Road, Theale, Reading, RG7 4AQ, UK. Tel: +44(0) 118 9306060; Fax: +44(0) 118 9302143; Email: info@integralis.co.uk; Website: www.integralis.co.uk

Managed security services

Before bringing in outside help to manage security services, run a series of checks first, says Stuart Eaton from Centrinet.

Economic and staff resourcing factors are further driving the trend for strategic outsourcing of specialist business areas – a fact noted by Allan Carey, senior analyst for IDC: 'The managed security services market is being driven primarily by resource constraints to capital and security expertise.'

This model however is not new; companies have previously outsourced functions such as legal matters, HR, recruitment, accounting and front desk security to outside specialists. The management of a company IT security infrastructure can be seen simply as an extension of this.

The 'managed service' market has burgeoned with the Internet security boom because of the financial and technical problems associated with a business attempting to stay ahead of the security curve. A report[1] by Morgan Chambers further suggested that there is evidence that outsourcing, as a strategic weapon, can have a positive impact on share price – the report suggests that the difference is about 5.3 per cent above the individual sector average and 4.9 per cent above the overall FTSE 100.

Managed security is not for everybody and we will outline the pros and cons of the strategy whilst providing pointers to what to look for in a managed security vendor.

---

[1] 'Outsourcing in the FTSE 100: The Definitive Study', Morgan Chambers.

Managed security pros

The benefits of outsourcing managed security include:

■ leveraging the talents and experience of security and privacy experts to protect brand, intellectual property and revenues;
■ supplementing existing security resources cost-effectively;
■ implementing sophisticated security solutions;
■ focusing resources on building core business, not on building a security centre or on trying to constantly stay on top of changing security threats;
■ controlling and managing security spending;
■ accessing a trusted advisor during security incidents;
■ obtaining third-party validation and verification of the appropriateness of your security policies;
■ benefiting from cutting-edge security research and development.

Managed security cons

Amongst the disadvantages of outsourcing security solutions we find:

■ allowing a third party access to the 'keys to the safe';
■ long term- inflexible contract terms;
■ that several companies in the managed security area are start-ups with an uncertain economic future;
■ trust as the main barrier.

Moving to the managed model

Once a decision is taken to embrace managed security how do you select a service provider? There are several key metrics to be checked off when searching for a good quality MSP (managed service provider):

■ written service-level agreements (SLAs);
■ secure financial position;
■ recognised standards, eg ISO;
■ global reach;
■ high level of vendor accreditations;
■ secure NOC (network operations centre);
■ customer testimony.

Let us deal with each of the above points separately.

Written service-level agreements (SLAs)

The primary objective of a managed security service is to provide security services that meet the agreed business and technical requirements of the client. To facilitate this, the service provider needs to understand these requirements and translate them into measurable criteria. This allows the service provider to measure the service delivered as well as its capability and performance in providing the service. This is typically done by the use of SLAs. SLAs are a key component as they outline the shared goals and objectives of the supplier and client; without them it is all too easy for the expectations of one party to fall out of line with those of the other, leading to a breakdown in both the relationship and service.

Secure financial position

After taking the time to select a suitable supplier of managed services, the last thing you want to happen is that they go bankrupt after a few months of the contract, leaving you 'high and dry'. Secure finances is perhaps the most important area to consider, even more so in the current economic climate. Part of the selection process here should be a check on the customer base and the length of time the company has operated within the managed service arena.

Managed services, as with many areas of IT, has seen a proliferation of start-up companies with a poor commercial model that leads to the disillusionment of their client base and, therefore, ultimately leading to disillusionment in the managed service model. This need not be the case if care is taken when partnering with a provider.

An interesting point in the financial area is that size is not always everything, as the recent WorldCom episode has demonstrated.

Recognised standards

If a company, particularly a service provider in this case, is awarded an ISO 9000 certificate, it can demonstrate to its customers that it is in possession of a documented quality system that is being observed and continually followed. ISO 9000 standardises the services of the company or organisation. One of the benefits of obtaining an ISO certificate is that the company is distinguished as a supplier of superior quality services and can display their commitment to a quality product. Partnering with a managed service provider that has made this investment in international standards allows us to have increased confidence in the products and services supplied. Assurance of conformity can be provided ordinarily by manufacturers' declarations or by audits carried out by an independent agency.

Global reach

A correctly scaled managed firewall or VPN (virtual private network) service allows companies to take advantage of the inherent benefits of a well-designed, secure firewall deployment within their enterprise. Further to this, partnering with a service provider that can boast current global deployments gives us the flexibility to expand outside of our home country without the headache of understanding the creation of a secure communications platform. Without this global reach we are in danger of missing out on the intrinsic and compulsive benefit of IP (Internet protocol) VPN, which is that it's a simple way to securely connect outlying sites. Having this power enables the rapid deployment of tactical offices and can further the facilitation of teleworking. An MSP with global reach will also have knowledge of global support and the ability to liaise, and at times manage, multi-ISP (Internet service provider) relationships.

Care should always be taken to partner with an MSP that allows your business to realise its growth potential and not hinder it through poor global experience.

Vendor accreditation

The vendor accreditation aspect again links back to an MSP's investment in the service they supply. Good levels of accreditation with the software or hardware vendor they manage will give the MSP a level of access to the vendor's R&D function, Beta programs and early release software. In turn, this allows the MSP to fully develop their offering and to ensure that they are not caught out by service or feature pack updates that may have an impact on the security of the service.

In attaining a level of accreditation, an MSP is required to meet specified standards and program protocols; these may include a minimum level of accredited and trained staff or a target number of customers subscribing to the service. Once again, when looking for a suitable service provider, accreditations and/or ISO standards give a good indication of the level of service you can expect to receive.

Secure NOC (network operations centre)

When outsourcing the management of your firewalls/intrusion detection systems to an MSP, a minimum component must be that they have a secure operations centre from which they can monitor, manage and administer your firewalls. When looking into any managed service contract, a trip to see the NOC should be a consideration. A good NOC should contain elements of CCTV, card readers and airlock door configurations in their security make-up. This ensures that only authorised staff will have access to key information.

A well-conceived, secure NOC is a strong indication that the service provider takes security seriously. This is one of *the* key metrics when selecting a partner.

Customer and industry testimony

An MSP that conforms to most, if not all, of the points raised above is likely to have a mature installed user base that can vouch for its competence. Any managed service organisations that receive glowing references from both customers and industry peers are likely to make full use of them in corporate literature, websites and advertisements. MSPs are only too happy to let prospective customers see their testimonial sheets as it gives a valuable comfort factor and can often be a crucial element in developing the trust that has to exist prior to embarking on a managed service contract.

Customer case studies and testimony can allow prospective clients to view the type of implementations a given MSP has been successful in deploying. It can also be an indicator of the vertical markets an MSP has experience in. This can be particularly important within certain sectors such as government or military.

Conclusion

Outsourcing security technologies is an increasing trend and one that seems set to continue. It is one of the fastest growing markets in the IT sector with more than US$250 million of venture capital funded US managed security start-ups in the last year. IDC expects the global market for security services to grow to US$16.5 billion by 2004 from US$4.8 billion in 1998.

When looking to utilise the skills of an MSP, companies should take the time to investigate vendors thoroughly. With the right choice, an MSP is a business partner who can shoulder the responsibility of an organisation's security management and incident response, thus enabling the company to operate confidently in today's connected business environment.

Centrinet are a leading provider of Internet and network security solutions based on the innovative use of the best products and services. Our passion for customer service and technical excellence, combined with a no-nonsense approach to business, provides our clients with a refreshing and unique experience.

For further information contact: Centrinet Limited, Witham Park House, Waterside South, Lincoln, Lincolnshire LN5 7JN. Tel +44 (0)1522 559 600; Fax: +44 (0)1522 533 745; Email: enquiries@centri.net; Website: www.centri.net

Security testing

Companies should not rely on customers to point out their faults, says Roy Hills of NTA Monitor.

How often do we hear in the news about customers finding faults in e-commerce websites and the negative publicity it brings? Yet we still find ourselves saying 'if our e-commerce system isn't working, our customers will soon let us know'. Relying on customers to test your system is the best way to lose them.

Security testing can be non-invasive or exploitative, depending on the client's requirements. Solutions range from fully automated scanning to semi-automated penetration testing to manual probing of websites and systems. Whichever method your company chooses, regular security testing to ensure prevention rather than cure is imperative.

Banking and e-commerce customers are often the first to notice when things go wrong, even before the website's IT staff and long before directors and senior management.

E-commerce customers are often headline news for being unable to access their own accounts, being presented with other users' personal details or finding credit card lists online. When this happens, their confidence in your service – so important when you are asking them to commit their own personal and financial details to cyberspace – can rapidly wane, along with your profits.

Such problems are not confined to the consumer arena. Commercial, legal and industrial firms often share clients' confidential data, plans and proposals online, in an insecure environment leaving them vulnerable to outsiders. The loss of client confidence can spread like a cancer if not checked.

An insecure website can also be costly. Eli Lilly, a drug maker, accidentally revealed the email addresses of 669 patients taking Prozac, an anti-depressant, which resulted in expensive out-of-court settlements.

A breach in online e-commerce security that results in accidental or unlawful disclosure of personal records will constitute a breach of Principle 7 of the Data Protection Act 1998. The result? Individuals and companies will be able to make a clear claim for compensation for damage suffered as a result of bad data processing practice.

Business can be lost in the short-term, but most importantly reputations can be permanently damaged.

Sometimes security problems arise during internal system changes by IT staff, but often it is the result of something more malicious, such as hackers testing their 'cyber-muscles' in order to deny user access, or those with more sinister, criminal intent. Recently, details of over a million credit cards were taken by Eastern European hackers when they penetrated around 40 e-commerce websites.

The more subtle attackers may gain access and do nothing to draw attention to their presence. Hacker 'toolkits' can be hidden within existing data. Changes may not be noticed for months.

Vulnerabilities to such attacks may appear in previously watertight systems whenever the systems are internally upgraded or reconfigured. Even adding a firewall can lead to other vulnerabilities. Few IT systems these days are static. Any change to the system might herald a change in its security.

Network security is something none of us can afford to compromise. Valuable IT time and resources may be required to recover systems, business can be lost in the short-term, but most importantly reputations can be permanently damaged.

While most off-the-shelf systems are extensively tested, many larger organisations prefer to design and build their own, although such bespoke systems are especially vulnerable. They are often complex and it is difficult to be sure that the system is working correctly, even though you have looked at all of the components and fitted them together properly. Regular penetration testing can help you to know your system's vulnerabilities and to do something about them before any trouble arrives.

Penetration testing demonstrates best practice – something increasingly important to professional indemnity insurance.

You might ask yourself how well you know your system, particularly if changes are made on a regular basis by different IT staff. Have all parts of the system been optimally secured? Have instructions been implemented properly? Could recent changes lead to new gaps? How will you know? Ongoing testing highlights any weaknesses and enables staff to make continual improvements.

So how is security testing carried out?

'*Regular Monitor*' penetration testing involves NTA looking at the vulnerability of a network from the point of view of a potential attacker and searching for any weakness that could be exploited to gain access to a system. However, this is done within very strict parameters. Security holes are located, identified and reported, but they are not exploited. Penetration testing effectively acts like exploratory surgery. In addition to testing the physical network, they also perform '*Internet Real-estate Mapping*', where they search for all the domain names allocated to your site. They also search for similar domain names that could be used to host rogue e-commerce sites, which dupe unsuspecting users into submitting their password and credit card details to a site they believe is yours. A scam of this type has been targeted at eBay, the online auction site. NTA use unique test engines that run a huge number of tests quickly, ensuring the whole process is normally complete within a couple of days.

Penetration testing acts like exploratory surgery. Security holes are located, identified and reported, but never exploited.

Once a client has been tested using the penetration method, often they wish to explore their security further and take on the more exploitative option of manual probing. This solution involves a qualified technician manually trying to exploit a system for flaws and to either gain deeper access into the network or to achieve a 'denial of service' if possible. Clients are assured of the utmost confidentiality, so even given the nature of the testing, their reputation and private data are not at risk.

Security testing gives operators greater confidence in their systems and gives their customers greater trust, safe in the knowledge that data and communications are secure. Never let the customer be the one to inform you that things are going wrong. To put your Internet customers first, first regularly check your system.

NTA Monitor was set up in 1997 as an Internet security specialist organisation and has now become Europe's leading security tester. The length of its blue-chip client list demonstrates its success in delivering quality services effectively.

NTA Monitor's customer base across seven countries includes over 300 clients, spanning all industries, from banking and finance through to pharmaceuticals, motor manufacturers, retailers, law firms, the food industry and including central and local government.

NTA Monitor has been a founding member since January 1999 of the UK Government CESG 'CHECK' security tester certification scheme, and has provided testing to government departments for the UK Government Secure Intranet (GSI) and similar projects in other countries.

For further information contact: NTA Monitor Ltd, 14 Ashford House, Beaufort Court, Medway City Estate, Rochester, Kent ME2 4FA. Tel: +44 (0)16324 721 855; Fax: +44 (0)1634 721 844; Email: marketing@nta-monitor.com

Open source in the enterprise

Paul Smeddle at the The Positive Internet Company considers the advantages of Open Source software for ensuring the integrity of your business online.

Allow this chapter to be your final notice: if your business relies on proprietary software, you are living on borrowed time. This might seem an overblown claim. Indeed, you might not even be aware of what constitutes proprietary software. If so, it's time to reconsider carefully upon what foundation the whole information infrastructure of your organisation is founded. Firstly, a simple definition. Proprietary software is, these days, the usual sort of software you pull off the shelf and agonise over licensing seats and the like. You install it, it goes wrong, you complain, you pay for the upgraded product, it goes wrong again, and the whole cycle continues ad infinitum. Or at least, ad insanity, if you're trying to keep up with the licensing machinations of the larger software manufacturers.

In proprietary software, a single company claims 'ownership' of the software, and keeps a tight grip on its 'intellectual property'. Often part of the 'intellectual property' they so carefully guard is the nature of that 'intellectual property' itself. By refusing either to open their standards or in fact to use existing open standards, many companies adhere to a policy of security through obscurity, whereby nothing at all is made public about the way the software works, particularly with regard to security issues. Wait, I hear you cry, isn't that a good thing? The unequivocal answer is no. This may seem counter-intuitive, but bears closer scrutiny. If a company builds a bank safe and declares it secure, it means nothing unless the safe has passed independent testing at the hands of some disinterested standards body. Sadly, in the software industry, this can rarely happen. What's more, imagine if you purchased a bank safe and were told that to test its security and probe its vulnerabilities even after legally buying one was illegal.

Software companies are prone to selling solutions that are declared secure by those who build them. This is a ludicrous state of affairs. Clearly such software needs to be tested independently. The best way to test the technical strengths and weaknesses of a product is to open it up to public scrutiny. Indeed, this is the basis of the scientific method. Peer review, full disclosure and the likes are the kingpin of our scientific culture. As there is virtually no incremental cost in distributing software for wide testing, it is possible to expose a product to a huge number of people, some of whom have the top technical skills in the industry, including perhaps those working for rival companies with a vested interest in detecting flaws. Software exposed to this pack of wolves must pass muster or be sent packing. Unfortunately, it is not in many large companies' interests to have their flagship software product's security trashed by a Scandinavian computer science professor, so they try ever harder, through increasingly brutal copyright legislation and the like, to sweep things under the corporate-secrecy carpet.

This affects the consumer directly, as the market is diluted with vendors selling virtual 'snake oil remedies', at least as far as security is concerned. This may sound cynical, perhaps even alarmist, but the truth is that many vendors are earnestly selling products with flawed security models, in the belief that obfuscation and intellectual property battles are sufficient and necessary to protect their code.

The security community at large has a long history of taking matters into its own hands in a virtual 'name and shame' tradition, where security flaws in many products, commercial or otherwise are openly discussed. One such forum is the 'bugtraq' list, a security mailing list that any one can subscribe to. Bugtraq has gained a certain amount of notoriety in some sectors of the software industry and the IT press for its policy of publishing the unexpurgated details of security exploits as soon as they are discovered. This has led to criticism from several large companies who find themselves either unable or unwilling to publish patches for vulnerable code as fast as is needed. It has been deemed 'irresponsible' by these entities, but has been defended rigorously by renowned security experts such as Bruce Schneier, author of one of the most popular cryptography manuals, and inventor of several widely-used encryption algorithms.

In his popular monthly Internet newsletter, 'Crypto-Gram', Schneier comments on a draft IETF specification, which would require the vendor to be alerted of any exploit in advance of its publication. He agrees with the idea in principle, but warns that companies could use the procedure to withhold information about vulnerabilities in their software. Indeed, he notes that the threat of full-disclosure of a wide-spread SNMP bug was the primary motivator in convincing companies to patch their faulty software.

Open Source software avoids these pitfalls by simultaneously being completely transparent in terms of its security models, and providing security experts who discover flaws with the means to develop patches for these flaws immediately. Open Source software is described by Eric Raymond in the 'Jargon File' as 'software distributed in source under licences guaranteeing anybody rights to freely use, modify, and redistribute the code'.

Simply put, this means that anyone who buys or otherwise obtains an Open Source product also gets the 'source code', or programmer-level (as opposed to machine-level) instructions in which the software package was written. This allows anyone who has the product to audit it for security, raising the alarm if a vulnerability is discovered. Furthermore, they can write a fix for the vulnerability, perhaps in consultation with the original authors or other technically adept users of the product. This fix can then be examined and audited, in turn, by the larger user community. This achieves the twin aims of peer review and full disclosure by which systems are ratified, advanced and secured.

Such full and open discussion of security models does generate a lot of traffic in security forums on the subject of vulnerabilities, which may be misinterpreted by the casual (or in some cases disingenuous) observer as evidence for Open Source software's inherent insecurity. On the contrary, such healthy and rapid-fire analysis and discussion is what keeps Open Source software consistently ahead of the curve in terms of security. With proprietary software, undisclosed vulnerabilities can exist for months or even years, and even fixes for known vulnerabilities are often issued less promptly than they could be. Open Source software, especially software that is freely distributed such as the Linux kernel and the GNU operating system of which it usually forms a part, often has a patch for a vulnerability available in conjunction with the initial announcement of said vulnerability.

Much has been said recently about the 'total cost of ownership' of Open Source systems. Some of the claims levelled against them are that they require highly-trained people to configure and manage them, are inherently complex and are incompatible with some commercial vendors' offerings. The fact of the matter is that system security rests as much on the people administering the software as it does on the software. Proprietary or otherwise, there is no panacea for all your security concerns, and there is unlikely to be an entirely secure piece of software, ever. Therefore, spending money on software at the expense of people skills is an inherently misguided impulse, especially when the (arguably) most secure software is often available for free (for most free software is Open Source, but the reverse is not true). The compatibility issues often cited are the result of the use of proprietary standards and protocols for the most part, which detract from the overall security of products that use them.

Therefore, Open Source software is often cheaper (or free). You can't afford to skimp on human resources if you take security seriously, and compatibility issues are a red herring. Weighed up against the very real costs of seat licences, upgrades, deprecated product lines and being at the mercy of the vendor for security updates, Open Source software looks to be the only option for those who are serious about their data.

The Positive Internet Company is the leading Linux-only webhosting company. They have a strong reputation in all aspects of Internet security, intrusion detection and Open Source solutions.

For further information contact: The Positive Internet Company Ltd, 24 Broadway, London W13 0SU. Tel: +44 (0)20 8579 5551; Freephone: (UK only) 0800 316 1006; Fax (UK only) 07020 935 412; Email: good@positive-internet.com; Website: www.positive-internet.com

Organisational back-up

Watching us, Watching you...

Your greatest fear is losing control

Augmenta from Internetworking Strategies takes away the worry of managing your network security, but keeps you involved and informed. The Augmenta secure web portal shows the customer how we're performing in real time - 24 hours a day.

Monitoring services, not just firewalls

Augmenta takes a wider view - looking beyond your firewalls to the services they support - monitoring both network equipment and servers to make sure your business runs reliably and securely - 24 hours a day.

Augmenta listens

The Augmenta portal also lets you talk to us - via a secure web interface to our fault and change management systems - listening to you and providing feedback in real time - 24 hours a day.

@ugmenta
The Interactive Managed Service

brought to you by

insl
internetworking strategies ltd

Employee confidentiality and a culture of security

The best way to ensure employee security is to make them aware of the risks, writes Peter Wilson from Tarlo Lyons Solicitors.

Along with the commercial advantages that the increased use of e-commerce has had, there is an ever-increasing number of security issues that arise. Global interaction and interconnectivity mean that customers are more accessible to providers, but it also means that the business is more vulnerable to everyone. Failure to properly deal with information security issues involves both regulatory risk (such as data protection) and more general business risk.

Recent statistics suggest that almost half of UK businesses suffer at least one malicious security breach a year. The average cost of a serious security breach is £30,000. Despite the growing threat, only 27 per cent of UK businesses spend more than one per cent of their total IT budget on information security.[1]

Although there are hundreds of security products now available on the market, there is one defence that outstrips the rest in terms of both value for money and effectiveness: namely, awareness. Linked to this is the creation of a culture of security and the need to bind staff to contracts that protect the business's trade secrets and confidential information.

---

[1] DTI *Information Security Breaches Survey 2002*.

Security awareness and employees

Managers and directors of businesses need to be aware of the threats facing their organisations and of the potentially devastating effect that a security breach could have on them. They also need to be aware that there are a number of simple steps that can be taken to enhance security.

One of the biggest threats to information security that a company is faced with comes from its own employees. In order to minimise this risk, a culture of security should be promoted within companies; this begins as early as the recruitment process.

Recruitment, contracts and policies

Even if the recruitment function is outsourced, it is still the end-user's business that is at risk, so it is the end-user who must ensure that both the method of recruitment and the contract governing the outsourcing cover the issue of security:

■ background checks should be carried out on all staff and potential staff;
■ the employee should be made aware of his/her obligations, both under the contract of employment, and through office-wide policies;
■ a strong password must be used and changed on a regular basis to keep the network more secure;
■ if employees work from home, or remotely via laptops, dual identification procedures should be used.

Along with all of the issues relating to information security, managers should keep in mind the regulation of employees' human rights and data protection issues, which impact on data storage and employee surveillance.

If any of the company's business is conducted online, especially where money transactions take place on the Internet, information coming in from external sources should be checked twice: once as information is fed between the external source and the website; and once as it moves between the website and the company network. This is especially important when dealing with overseas customers, because regulation of information security may not be as stringent as it is in the UK. If dealing with international websites on a more permanent basis – ie if a business function has been outsourced overseas – it is important that the contracts governing the movement of information between the two sites deal with the issues of information security and data protection, and that they provide an equivalent level of protection to the laws in the UK.

As well as awareness of the threats facing the company, management should ensure that there are procedures, and accountable people throughout the management structure, in place to deal with a security breach should it happen. Early detection can save thousands of pounds worth of damage to the network. As new viruses are introduced every week, the virus software that covers a company's network should be updated regularly. Having a back-up server can cut down the downtime for web-based products, thus minimising the loss of business and customer confidence. Another way to safeguard customer confidence is to ensure that publicity is handled carefully.

Employment contracts

A carefully drafted employment contract can help secure the following:

- the employee's compliance with the relevant security procedures and policies;
- compliance with the employer's email and Internet policies;
- protection of the business's intangible assets: copyright, databases, inventions, trade secrets and confidential information (including customer lists and technical information such as computer source code). This can be achieved through the use of restrictive covenants where appropriate. Also, express clauses protecting these assets can be included, which ensure that a higher level of protection is granted than that given by law.

Conclusion

IT spending has increased as the advantages of e-commerce have been recognised by UK businesses; but the spending on IT security is still worryingly low. The publicity surrounding international incidents such as the Melissa and Lovebug viruses shows just how vulnerable businesses and national infrastructure systems are to cyber-criminals. Company directors are beginning to acknowledge that the risks associated with providing e-commerce services are some of the most serious facing businesses today, and yet the most basic measures are still not being implemented. Businesses must implement security policies and appropriate technologies both to comply with data protection law and to protect their operations.

Tarlo Lyons is a leading London law firm focused on delivering commercial solutions for technology-driven business. It has one of the largest teams of dedicated technology lawyers in England, and believes in leveraging the expertise and talent it has assembled to provide real benefits for its clients. It believes that success comes from contributing to its client's objectives, and its ability to understand and work with technology is central to this.

For further information contact: Tarlo Lyons, Watchmaker Court, 33 St. John's Lane, London EC1M 4DB. Tel: +44 (0)20 7405 2000; Fax: +44 (0)20 7814 9421; Website: www.tarlolyons.com

Electronic contracting

The errors that result from computers making contracts differ from the ones made by people, says William Kennair, Chair, ICC's (International Chamber of Commerce) Commission on E-Business, IT and Telecoms Task Force on Security and Authentication. Legal rules relating to mistake, bad faith and misrepresentation may not fit the errors that result from computers processing transactions.

'Electronic contracting' is the automated process of entering into contracts via the contracting parties' computers, whether networked or through electronic messaging. Because the parties can program their computers to respond automatically to certain inputs (such as an offer or enquiry), the parties may not be aware in every case of precisely what their networked computers are doing, and they may not consciously participate in the contract formation process. Moreover, the errors that result from computers making contracts (probably due to the programming logic) are sometimes not the kind that human beings would make, and the legal rules relating, for example, to mistake, bad faith and misrepresentation may not quite fit the errors that result from computers processing transactions.

The economic context in which electronic contracting takes place has come to be dominated by large-scale public networks of computers – networks that have become easy to use and practically ubiquitous in many commercial environments, for example, the World Wide Web. These developments fundamentally affect the way business is done, even where it is already being done electronically. The greater power and reach of the new networks also offer opportunities for achieving greater efficiency in performing transactions. To consider how transactions work electronically, a look at basic business models is informative.

Electronic business models

In most economic cultures the basic model for doing business is the market. In a market model, those who *have* meet those who *need* – they bargain and agree, and they exchange. The market is assumed to operate among an open, broad community, and in that respect it differs from a chain. This constitutes an open business model.

In a chain, the number of buyers and sellers is restricted due to obligations of exclusivity. If a chain has been imposed, a stranger can no longer simply go to the marketplace and sell what he has or buy what he needs. Instead, a seller is committed to sell only to a specified buyer or small group of buyers. Similarly, a buyer is also restricted to a defined set of sellers. This constitutes a closed business model. The exclusivity is a matter of degree and depends, among other things, on:

■ *Relative bargaining power of the parties.* The relative number and availability of alternatives are amongst the factors determining bargaining power. Bargaining power has often proven to be greater in the buying role, assuming that many potential suppliers exist or can be induced to exist.
■ *Cost of building one-off relationships.* The stranger-to-stranger transactions of the market model can be expensive, depending on how the transactions are carried out.

In the recent past, the cost of building relationships has increasingly led those parties with superior bargaining power to promote the building of chains. Factors that contribute to that cost are:

■ *Need for specialised goods.* In the automotive, aerospace and similar industries, the captive supply chain manufactures goods that are not standard, fungible commodities but rather are made to the buyer's specifications. Over time the supplier may recover the costs of tooling-up to produce goods that satisfy unique specifications, and may thus become economically dependent on a powerful buyer. In addition to specialised goods, distribution services are often established to support the chains and are dependent on the chains for their subsequent survival.
■ *Technical set-up and integration.* Traditional electronic data interchange (EDI) is based on the chain model because of the difficulty and complexity of setting up interconnected databases and reliable means of transferring information between them. The legal approach to EDI reinforced this dependence on chains – the legal basis for EDI was established bilaterally between 'trading partners' through an agreement that was intended to suffice for all transactions that the parties would carry out. EDI has thus greatly promoted the development of trade chains in recent years at the expense of free choice in the marketplace.

A more recent model is the web portal, whereby an intermediary establishes favourable pricing for purchases made through their portal. Generally they establish a closed user-consumer/retail group, and membership involves agreeing to certain rules. This model is between a closed and open system, being less formally structured than EDI, and is business-to-consumer focused rather than business-to-business focused as in EDI. The technical connectivity is much simpler and the relationship is established contractually. Other forms of 'portal' are appearing that are aimed at providing an open marketplace or exchange of goods and services. This marketplace or exchange is itself a service, and the growth of intermediaries is an indication of the major change from more traditional business models.

Although chains have become common in recent years, the market (or 'open') model retains a great advantage over the chain (or 'closed') model and a modest advantage over the semi-closed portal model: it is more economically efficient. The exclusivity of a chain causes the buyer to forego getting it cheaper elsewhere and the seller to forego finding a better price elsewhere. A chain also burdens innovation by locking in a defined set of suppliers and locking out entrepreneurs with innovative products but without access to the locked-in sales channel. Further, a market is also highly responsive to changing circumstances, whereas the complexity and production integration of a chain can make it slow to realise that, for example, cars must now be more fuel-efficient. Fundamentally, the economic attractiveness of the market model persists.

Early electronic commerce fostered the proliferation of chains into areas where either they had not existed or they had never been firmed up into legal commitments. EDI was so difficult and complex to set up that it required the co-operation of both buyer and seller. Securing that co-operation often involved a strong party compelling a weaker one to join in the interchange. However, the cost savings possible through EDI made the economic inefficiency of the chain model compared to the market model tolerable. However, as electronic commerce matures, it becomes simpler, easier and more standardised, as well as more powerful. It has also become nearly ubiquitous, more than widely enough distributed to support a market model of commerce. These subsequent developments create opportunities for increased economic efficiency by re-evaluating where a chain is necessary and where a return to a market model can yield advantage.

It is important to remember, however, that whatever model is in use, the protocols or systems in use must be fit for purpose and the controls in place must be appropriate to the value of the transaction.

Developments affecting economic models

The developments since the early days of electronic commerce (the EDI era) have reduced much of the technical complexity and interdependence required to engage in electronic commerce. Today, many parties without extraordinary technical sophistication buy and sell electronically at a cost of set-up unimaginable in the EDI days. In large measure, this change is a result of:

- more powerful yet user-friendly methods of information interchange;
- the commercialisation of trust, and
- electronic contracting.

The following section examines each of those in turn.

More powerful messages

The information-carrying power and flexibility of electronic messages has increased dramatically in recent years. In early electronic commerce, messages consisted merely of unlabelled data fields in a prescribed form. Because development and set-up for utilising those messages was laborious and expensive, software producers and system integrators insisted on widespread agreement on all aspects of the form, which meant that the form became inflexible. While this highly formalised approach to electronic commerce remains common in older systems, a new approach to message form has emerged from the World Wide Web. Experience with hypertext markup language (HTML), the format for Internet documents derived from the standard generalised markup language (SGML), led to making SGML extensible, and the extensible markup language (XML) was born. XML has since overtaken the earlier formalistic messages used in EDI, although EDI remains in use in legacy systems. The power and flexibility of newer message forms and their ability to integrate data with a documentary context sets the stage functionally for electronic contracting. Besides these functional capabilities, business-grade electronic commerce requires message security and assured authenticity.

Commercialisation of trust

All forms of trade require an essential element of trust between the participants. As we move towards using the Internet for electronic trading (electronic commerce), this ability to trust must be maintained. For centuries a significant element of trading has been the ability to carry out transactions in a confidential manner and to be able to 'bind' the resultant deal. This may have been in the form of a handshake, or by signed and witnessed documents. Some transactions are anonymous, whilst some only require the exchange of a token such as a bond or a Bill of Lading. Whatever the process, the electronic environment must enable it to continue.

Trust is an abstract quality that is generally derived over time between two (or more) parties. Within electronic contracting the parties may not have met, and there is a desire to 'fast-track' the establishment of an appropriate level of trust. Consequently, the ability to rely on an electronic message has become progressively commercialised as an industry that is increasingly known by the term 'trust services'. The value of trust services lies in a transfer of risk from the parties in a transaction to third-party service providers. For example, the following services are commonly used in business-grade electronic commerce:

■ *Authenticity services* ensure that a message is genuine – in other words, that it is authenticated by an identified party, that it has remained intact and that evidence can be produced to establish both of those facts should the sender deny authenticity. A 'certifier' as defined in the GUIDEC[1] is a species of authenticity service.
■ *Payment and credit services* ensure that instructions or obligations to pay are properly approved by the payer and carried out in favour of the intended payee. Some of these services are electronic adaptations of transactions originally developed on paper, such as bankcard charges and letters of credit. They also include experiments in new forms of electronic funds transfers.
■ *Operational auditing or accreditation services* review the security, information flows and other technical aspects of a system's operations to determine whether they accord with its obligations.

---

[1] General Usage for International Digitally Ensured Commerce.

These commercial trust services supporting business-grade electronic commerce create a basis for conducting transactions that is at least as solid as the traditional paper basis. Together with more powerful message capabilities, they make electronic contracting possible on a scale greater than previously envisaged.

Automated and agent-based electronic contracting

Networked computers make and perform contracts with increasing frequency using the various business models described above. They also perform other actions that can greatly affect the rights and liabilities of the parties. The active, conscious participation of the parties in these processes can vary from a thorough deliberation about the legal significance of a transaction to complete unawareness. These new electronic contracting capabilities introduce a new dynamic into business and trade transactions. It is now easy to make contracts, because parties can automate the contract formation process and then manage it much like they manage their other critical information technology systems.

The ease of making contractual deals through automation may lead prevailing commercial structures back towards market economic models. Extensive networks such as the Internet and NASDAQ have demonstrated the vitality of markets in which highly-customised products are not the object. Markets, rather than chains, are the natural and more efficient economic model in large networks where the many who *have* are juxtaposed against the many who *need*.

Besides enabling a return to market economics, automated (including agent-based) electronic contracting can also potentially be more flexible. It can facilitate better alignment with the real relationship between the parties as it evolves. In the thought under-lying EDI and chains, contract formation was viewed as a manual process that occurred once and for all when a link in the chain was forged. This front-loading of the contract formation process made the transactional rules incapable of evolving as the relationship evolved and incapable of responding to new opportunities or transactions. Setting out ground rules at the start makes sense, but ground rules should leave room for working out contractual specifics later. It is more practical to have an initial enabling contract that sets out ground rules and to allow further contracts to draw in specific details, opportunities, transactions and relationships that occur. In particular, those later, more specific contracts can perhaps most efficiently be made through automated electronic contracting.

Principles of fair electronic contracting (POFEC)

The first GUIDEC set the stage for a principled commercialisation of trust in accordance with business needs, and now by incorporating principles of fair electronic contracting (POFEC), the current version seeks to do the same for electronic contracting. Although electronic contracting offers new possibilities for efficient transactions and economics, as well as greater flexibility and evolutionary capabilities, it also has new vulnerabilities that can be abused and could face theoretical validity questions in some legal systems.

Abuse may arise because the capabilities of computers in processing documents have limitations that are different from those of people. A computer's ability to perceive the significance of information depends entirely on what its programming anticipates and what the computer can recognise in its input. It would, for instance, have great difficulty in ascer-taining a price from a simple, untagged expression that would be quite clear to a human reader, such as 'for a price of ten pounds sterling per dozen'.

Further, even if the input is tagged to make it recognisable to a computer, a program may fail to properly interpret and process it. Usually such short-sightedness in programming is inadvertent or simply a constraint to be accommodated; but failings can also result from pranks, or from even more sinister causes. However, although a computer's document processing capabilities are limited and susceptible to abuse, many business leaders are finding that the speed and cost savings of automation nevertheless justify the use of computers to process business documents.

Increasingly, such documents can affect the obligations and rights of the computer users. Computers now perform transactions that cannot be seen as anything other than the making or extending of a contract. Sometimes those transactions are validated by an enabling umbrella agreement. However, contracts are also now commonly made between strangers via the Internet, without any ascertainable previous relationship between them at all, let alone a preparatory contract with provision for subsequent electronic contracting. The increasing commercial significance of the transactions that computers perform, despite their limitations and vulnerabilities, demands practices that respect those limitations and vulnerabilities.

The POFEC examine the computer-to-computer processing of commercial documents, and in particular those documents that cause non-consumers to incur or increase their obligations. They do not, and cannot, establish legal requirements themselves, but they do state best practices in order to inform on both policy and the practical conduct of international commerce as it proceeds to involve obligations incurred in ever-more automated ways.

The main elements of the POFEC are:

1. Drafting of documents for document processing systems to:

■ avoid a battle of forms;
■ incorporate external documents sparingly and carefully;
■ avoid inclusion of inapplicable text;
■ use document type when appropriate;
■ avoid unrecognisable mark-up in a document;
■ ensure authenticity adequately;
■ permit manual intervention and override.

2. Legal efficacy of electronic contracting covering:

■ assent by a document processing system;
■ mistakes and document processing systems;
■ availability of the human readable form;
■ principles of evidence.

It is anticipated that further projects within ICC's Commission on E-Business, IT and Telecoms will tackle in greater detail many of the issues raised herein.

ICC is *the* world business organisation and the only representative body that speaks with authority on behalf of enterprises from all sectors in every part of the world.

Because its member companies and associations are themselves engaged in international business, ICC has unrivalled authority in making rules that govern the conduct of business across borders. Although these rules are voluntary, they are observed in countless thousands of transactions every day and have become part of the fabric of international trade.

For more information on GUIDEC II contact: International Chamber of Commerce, 38 Cours Albert 1er, 75008 Paris, France. Tel: +33 1 49 53 30 13; Fax: +33 1 49 53 28 59; E-Business, IT and Telecoms email: ayesha.hassan@iccwbo.org; Website: www.iccwbo.org

Information security training

John Harrison from SAINT (Security Alliance for the Internet and New Technologies) takes a fresh look at some of the training issues in relation to security and provides advice on and an insight into what an organisation can do to effectively address their security training requirements.

Why is security training important?

This may sound like an obvious question, but it is important to look at what problems security training is likely to address effectively. Training is a 'people' issue – again, an obvious statement, but so often we overlook the obvious.

The SANS Institute conducted a survey in 1999 amongst 1,850 computer security experts and managers to identify the seven top management errors that lead to computer security vulnerabilities. At the top of this list they found that management 'assign untrained people to maintain security and provide neither the training nor the time to make it possible to do the job'.

Things have moved on since 1999, so we must be doing better than this – or are we? To allow you to judge, visit the SANS Institute website at www.sans.org/newlook/resources, where all seven errors are listed, and ask yourself: do any of these apply to my organisation?

The first key message, which is as true today as it was in 1999, is that information security training should involve everyone, and extend well beyond the needs of the IT department.

Closer to home and more recently, the DTI sponsored the *Security Breaches Survey 2002* (www.security-survey.gov.uk), which indicated that information security has never been a higher priority at the board level (73 per cent compared to 53 per cent in 2000), but relatively few businesses are translating this priority into effective action.

The survey went on to reveal the level of under-investment in IT security, with only 27 per cent of UK companies investing more than one per cent of their IT budget in security measures, whereas the global benchmark is three to five per cent. Perhaps the most telling result is that only 27 per cent of UK companies have a security policy, which is a fundamental aspect of good information security.

The survey includes advice on the top ten actions for the board, with the first bulleted item being to 'make sure your business creates a security-aware culture by educating staff about security risks and their responsibilities'. This is another endorsement for security training and awareness.

Security training and security awareness – what is the difference?

Information security is, above all, a business issue, which involves people, processes and technology. As already shown, many in the security industry would advise organisations wishing to improve their security that if they only have the resources to do one new thing, then they should be directed at 'security awareness'. But how does this differ from 'security training' and does it matter?

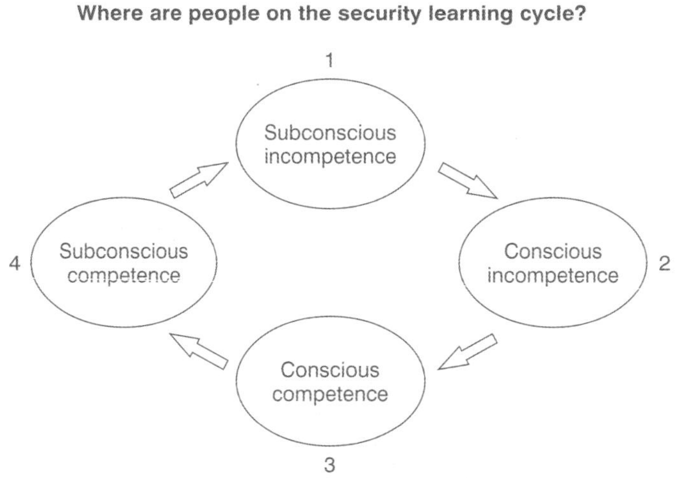

Where are people on the security learning cycle?

Figure 5.3.1 The 'learning cycle model'

To find out, we can look at some of the models that came out of the 'quality' drive in the 1980s. The 'learning cycle model' (see Figure 5.3.1) shows how a person moves from being subconsciously incompetent towards the goal of being subconsciously competent. Take, for example, riding a bike: people start by not being aware of whether they can ride or not (1), to falling off and realising they cannot (2), to getting their balance for the first time (3) to riding without thinking about it (4).

The most important point about this model is that as you move round from 1 to 4, each transition normally requires more effort than the one before – for example, moving from 1 to 2 can often be done quickly and with little effort. I would argue that 'security awareness' facilitates moving from 1 to 2; 'security training' facilitates moving from 2 to 3 and 'practice' facilitates moving from 3 to 4.

It is also worth noting that over time people move from 4 back to 1 as, particularly in the case of security, new vulnerabilities and countermeasures are continually evolving, hence the cliché: 'security is a journey not a destination'.

However, security awareness is about more than simply helping people realise there is a problem; it must also address motivational aspects to persuade people to take the next steps around the learning cycle.

The second model addresses the question: 'How do you get anyone to expend effort to change?' (see Figure 5.3.2). This shows that the second key message is that the relevance of information security training must be clear to both the individual and the employer.

This can be done in many ways, not least through the inclusion of information security within personal objectives and job descriptions that are tailored to the needs of the business.

To summarise, security awareness can be thought of as creating the aspiration, whilst security training can be seen as one important means of achieving this aspiration. They are complementary and both are necessary for creating a security-aware culture by helping people move round the security learning cycle.

Who should be trained, how, and what should they be trained in?

The answers to the 'who', 'how' and 'what' questions will depend on the individual and on the needs of your business, but the following points are relevant.

Who needs to be trained?

It is not glib to say that everyone in an organisation at some time or another should receive some sort of information security training. In some organisations it is not unusual for every employee to have a security-related item in their job description and, where appropriate, to have specific relevant personal objectives. I know of one organisation where over 80,000 employees had an objective to undergo security training, which for logistical and cost reasons was delivered by a combination of video and an interactive computer-based course, which was assessed and discussed at their annual appraisal.

How do you get anyone to expend effort to change?

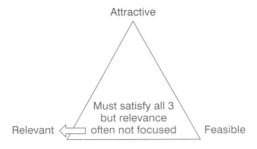

Figure 5.3.2 Encouraging change

The advice is, therefore, to examine your own organisational structure and to review the security training needs of each role within the business. To ensure relevance it is important to understand the 'what' aspect of training, which is discussed later.

How should the training be conducted?

One example of how to conduct the training has already been given where distance learning was used effectively. Training courses are also very effective, both external and in-house, and on some of the more technical training it is important to provide hands-on training facilities. There are many vendor-specific technical training courses, and consulting firms can be employed to run courses on almost any aspect of information security. In some cases, vendors provide road shows where they offer free training at various locations around the country, with a view to demystifying the security aspects of their products and, therefore, helping build trust and confidence in them.

Self-help training is facilitated by the numerous websites offering security guidelines, many of which are described and linked to the SAINT website at www.intellectuk.org/saint. A good example of self-help guidelines, written in plain English and primarily for the SME market, are the AEB web security guidelines, which can be found at www.intellectuk.org/publications/business_guidance_papers/web_sec_guidelines.pdf. These guidelines are complementary to ISO/IEC 17799 and provide a framework for developing and implementing effective security measures to manage the security risks that could affect a website and e-business processes. Another good example is the guide from the US National Cyber Security Alliance, which can be found at www.staysafeonline.info, again providing guidance in plain language for the cyber-citizen and small business.

How this training is managed is another important consideration, and a good vehicle for this would be within the general Investors in People standard being adopted by many organisations. Further information on this quality standard can be found at www.iipuk.co.uk.

What training is required?

This question is perhaps the most complex to deal with, as what training is required depends on the individual, their role within an organisation and the aspirations of both the individual and the organisation. A good starting point, however, is to look at possible structures for determining what training is needed.

A logical place to start would be to organise training around the 'information security policy' of the organisation, where, for example, all desktop users could be trained on the Internet usage policy. The major flaw in this approach is that, according to the DTI sponsored security survey, only 27 per cent of organisations have a security policy – so what about the remaining 73 per cent?

BS 7799 is another logical place to start, Part 1 of which is a code of practice for information security management. This was adopted in 2000 as an international standard ISO/IEC 17799. It describes a large number of controls that an organisation can adopt to safeguard the confidentiality, integrity and availability of its information.

Training based on the ten major sections of BS 7799 (Part 1) would provide a structure that would support the adoption of good information security practice within an organisation, noting that one of the major sections addresses the need to create security policies.

However, perhaps the most significant example of leadership in security comes from the OECD (Organisation for Economic Co-operation and Development) guidelines for the security of systems and networks, published in July 2002. These guidelines are aimed at promoting a culture of security and identify nine principles to help create this culture. It is worth noting that BS 7799 (Part 2) provides a process framework for implementing a number of these principles. These guidelines can be downloaded from the OECD website at www.oecd.org/pdf/M00033000/M00033182.pdf.

Given the scope of the OECD membership, and their position as a global authority, adoption of these nine principles must eventually be the long-term aim and aspiration of most organisations around the world.

This is the third time in this chapter that creating a culture of security has been a stated aim, and it is also the third key message, which is that any security training should play a part in creating a security-aware culture.

What training structure would be the most effective in the long term?

This section proposes that an effective structure for security training should be one that is based on the nine principles described in the OECD guidelines. These guidelines state that: 'All participants will be aided by awareness, education, information sharing and training that can lead to adoption of better security understanding and practices.'

The OECD guidelines are not detailed within this chapter, so it is recommended that the following section is read in conjunction with the guidelines (the nine principles are clear and concise, being described in three pages).

Principle 1 – Awareness

The need for security awareness has already been described in some detail within the opening sections of this document. The guidelines expand on the importance of risk awareness as the first line of defence and of people understanding the consequences arising from the abuse of information systems and networks.

Training should therefore ensure that people in all roles clearly understand these risks, and what they need to do to mitigate them.

Principle 2 – Responsibility

This has been touched on earlier in terms of including the relevance of information security within an individual's personal objectives and job description. The guidelines promote good management practices in terms of ensuring that individuals are aware of their responsibility and are accountable.

Training should therefore be provided to help ensure people have the necessary skills and knowledge for them to discharge this responsibility.

Principle 3 – Response

This recognises that security incidents will occur and that it is important to respond to them in a co-operative and timely manner. This raises an important point in terms of co-operation, because ideally training would need to inform on other people's misfortunes – that is, learning from other people's mistakes. However, information sharing is recognised as being difficult due to the potential loss of reputation arising from the risk of unsympathetic media reporting.

Training should therefore attempt to include content from shared information on sensitive issues such as incidents. The introduction of Information Sharing and Analysis Centres (ISACs) in the US is one attempt to do this (see https://www.it-isac.org) as an example within the IT sector.

Principle 4 – Ethics

This is fundamental to changing the culture in terms of making people recognise that their action or inaction may harm others. In the US, information security is now being taught at school level in order to change the perception that 'hacking is cool'. Organisations are also promoting ethical codes of conduct and the Institute of Directors (IoD), in particular, have published a code of ethics relating to information security.

Training should therefore be provided on codes such as these and delivered to all people in an organisation. A good place to start is induction training.

Principle 5 – Democracy

This can often be taken for granted in the UK, but it addresses the need for information security to be compatible with the essential values of a democratic society. One aspect of this relates to privacy and the right of a state to access information on an individual. Two pieces of UK legislation that relate to this aspect are the Data Protection Act 1998 and the Regulation of Investigatory Powers Act 2000.

Training should therefore be provided to help people understand the relevant legislation, both in terms of their rights and what is illegal.

Principle 6 – Risk assessment

Participants are encouraged to conduct risk assessments in this section of the guidelines. Risk is a term used by many but, arguably, understood by few. For example, what is the difference between risk assessment and risk management, and how do you undertake them?

Training should be given on risk and how it relates to the individual's role within the organisation. I would argue that this is a key topic and that it needs to be taught at all levels and to all roles within an organisation, as it is a prime mover towards a security-aware culture.

Principle 7 – Security design and implementation

I would argue that this is one of the most fundamental principles of the OECD guidelines where it states that systems, networks and policies need to be properly designed, implemented and co-ordinated to optimise security. I firmly believe that this offers one of the greatest opportunities for improvement as this principle is often neglected – evidenced by the DTI security survey, which stated 'Yet, only 14 per cent of UK businesses (32 per cent of large businesses) always document how security requirements are being addressed in the *design* of IT projects and 25 per cent (8 per cent of large businesses) never do'.

Training should be provided on how security can be designed into IT systems and networks, as well as on implementing and maintaining them in a secure manner. Suppliers and users should teach their staff how to do it, and clients should teach their staff how to procure systems and services that will be secure.

Principle 8 – Security management

The guidelines state that participants should adopt a comprehensive approach to security management. The obvious candidate on which this can be based is the BS 7799 code of practice for information security management, which is discussed briefly earlier in this chapter and elsewhere in this book.

Training should be provided against the background of the structure and approach for good information security management as described in BS 7799 Part 1 (ISO/IEC 17799:2000).

Principle 9 – Reassessment

This relates to the transition from stage 4 to 1 in the learning cycle described earlier, which reminds us that new and changing threats and vulnerabilities are continuously being discovered, prompting the need to continually review the appropriate countermeasures.

Security training should, therefore, not be a single event for any individual, but should be provided continuously to meet the needs of the changing environment. This also applies to security awareness, as it is important to continuously re-enforce the need for good security practice. Otherwise there is a risk of complacency, especially if no significant incidents occur.

Conclusion

It is recognised that not all the points of advice provided above will apply to everyone, but it is hoped that with the right prioritisation the reader can go away and act on at least one piece of advice or comment in this chapter. BS 7799 Part 1 offers the same approach in listing over 200 controls that can be adopted to ensure good information security management. However, it stresses that not all the controls will be relevant to all organisations.

In order to remain impartial, it is not appropriate for this book to recommend specific training packages. However there are many resources on the Internet that one can access for specific advice, including the vendor of the information systems used and the many public service sites, some of which are mentioned in this chapter.

There have been three key messages identified:

■ Information security training should involve everyone and extends well beyond the needs of the IT department.
■ The relevance of the information security training must be clear to both the individual and the employer.
■ Any security training should play a part in creating a security-aware culture.

These may seem obvious to many, but we are not always very good at doing the obvious when it comes to information security.

John Harrison advises on e-business security at Smart421 and works with Intellect, an ICT trade association with over 1000 members (www.intellectuk.org), and SAINT (Security Alliance for the Internet and New Technologies) in developing and promoting good practice in information security.

Smart421, as an active member of Intellect, has supported his work on many Intellect security projects, including the Alliance for Electronic Business (AEB) Web Security Guidelines and SAINT. John spent over a year developing SAINT before the prospectus was launched by the Minister for E-Commerce, and is now on the executive board of SAINT.

For further information contact: John Harrison, Associate, eBusiness Security, Smart421 (Smart solutions for the 21st century), North Felaw Maltings, 48 Felaw Street, Ipswich, Suffolk IP2 8HE. Tel: +44 (0)1473 421 421; Fax: +44 (0)1473 421 422; Mobile: +44 (0) 7860 425 321; Email: jharrison@smart421.com; Website: www.smart421.com

Beyond 'off the shelf'

Despite concerns about security, outsourcing can still make a lot of sense in the IT sector, writes Ken Watt from INSL.

Breaking with the past

Security has traditionally been something that organisations have kept close to their chests – an internal issue not to be entrusted to outsiders. In terms of physical security this instinct has softened over recent decades as contract guards, commercial alarm monitoring stations and secure couriers have taken the place of internal security services. Information and IT security, however, only began to embrace outsourcing very recently but its take-up is accelerating rapidly.

Outsourcing in IT security

Whilst general IT spend is under extreme pressure, security spend is widely predicted to maintain growth, with the outsourcing of services leading the way. By 2005, Gartner expects 60 per cent of US enterprises to outsource some form of perimeter security monitoring. Research by Forrester predicts that spending growth for outsource services will outstrip that of other security services by as much as 200 per cent over the same period. An Ernst and Young global information security survey in 2002 reported that 27 per cent of UK companies plan to outsource their security activities by the end of 2003.

Why the change?

This growth reflects changing attitudes as well as a need to control cost. In the background is an increasing awareness of security issues and the potential business impact of incidents – most significantly amongst senior and executive management. Whilst IT security used to be a fringe issue for specialists and 'geeks', it is now very much in the mainstream and has the attention of strategists and budget holders.

Underlying this growing awareness is a real increase in the level of incidents. CERT (the Computer Emergency Response Team – the leading global organisation for gathering and disseminating incident data) shows incident levels rose by over 200 per cent between 2000 and 2001 and by 300 per cent between 2000 and the third quarter of 2002. The DTI's Information Security Breaches Survey 2002 reports that hacking and virus attacks are costing £10 billion a year and that 78 per cent of large-cap companies have experienced some kind of electronic attack in the past year, with the average cost of a security breach at £30,000. Other industry surveys draw similar conclusions.

Identifying gaps

In a climate of sharply increasing risk an effective response is critical. Quite apart from questions over funding, organisations must assess the level and suitability of internal resources and whether existing staff can cope with the technical and operational demands of a growing and increasingly complex threat. Can a busy IT team give security adequate attention? If gaps exist, can the organisation find skilled and experienced staff and, if so, can it afford to hire them?

Surveys show consistently that, after budgetary constraints, companies see lack of skilled people as their most significant challenge. The range of expertise required in security often implies a breadth and depth of skill far beyond the means of all but the very largest companies. Discipline include risk assessment, policy and strategy, design, technical implementation, configuration and operations – covering firewalls and networks, applications and data security, desktops and user management and a host of other fields. The Forrester report referred to previously noted that nearly 50 per cent of companies surveyed saw lack of skilled people as a barrier to implementation of necessary security programmes.

Making the business case

Maintaining effective security requires very specialised skills, dedicated effort and, ideally, round-the-clock vigilance. This involves significant cost (hardware and software, ongoing software subscriptions, hardware maintenance, supplier technical support, staff training, monitoring operations support) across a range of equipment (firewalls, virus scanners, content filters, reporting tools, intrusion detection systems etc). Sadly, costs don't scale linearly with the size of company – so the choice for smaller companies is either to pay heavily for comprehensive security or to accept compromises.

Outsourcing can offer the economies of scale enjoyed by the largest companies in a package that is priced for the smaller organisation. For as little as the cost of half a full-time employee, it should be possible for a smaller organisation to have a fully managed and monitored perimeter security solution, with access to a team of specialists where necessary.

Here to stay

The world has moved on – information technology now pervades businesses of all sizes, so security has become a business rather than a technical issue. The complexity of both threat and response is leading companies to look outside for solutions. All the signs are that the outsource security market is here to stay and that its growth is set to continue over the coming years. The challenge for businesses is becoming one of supplier selection and management – something they ought to be more comfortable with.

INSL was founded in 1997 to fulfil a basic need in large and medium-sized enterprises for informed and practical advice on the safe connection of their networks to the Internet, to the networks of business partners, to other external networks and to their customers.

The company provides advice and help to customers on security policy, strategy and technical design, backed by practical skills in implementation and technical support. A carefully developed information security strategy is essential to any organisation, regardless of its size or the nature of its business. INSL provide qualified, experienced consultants and engineers for the design and implementation of security solutions in commercial environments. They are not only technicians but also experts in their field, capable of understanding the culture of the client's business and delivering appropriate security infrastructure and service.

For further information contact: Internetworking Strategies Ltd, 100 Preston Crowmarsh, Wallingford, Oxon OX10 6SL. Tel: +44 (0)1491 820900; Fax: +44 (0)1491 820 901; Email: info@insl.co.uk; Website: www. insl.co.uk

Contingency planning

Business continuity and crisis management

Dr David Smith FBCI from the Business Continuity Institute outlines various approaches that can help companies prepare for a business continuity 'event', and explains the BCM life-cycle.

In August 2002, the Financial Services Authority (FSA) expressed deep concern over the high percentage of its members who did not have a business continuity and/or crisis management capability. They emphasised that a robust, effective and fit-for-purpose preparedness is essential – and complacency is unacceptable – in the face of the challenges and threats that inevitably arise in today's business climate. This warning is reinforced by the recently published research report[1] of the Chartered Management Institute.

Business continuity management (BCM) is defined by the Business Continuity Institute (BCI) as 'an holistic management process that identifies potential impacts that threaten an organisation and provides a framework for building resilience and the capability for an effective response that safeguards the interests of its key stakeholders, reputation, brand and value creating activities'.

The BCI's use of the term 'business continuity management' rather than 'business continuity planning' is deliberate because 'planning' implies there is a start and end to the process and can lead to unwanted planning bureaucracy. BCM is, by necessity, a dynamic, proactive and ongoing process. It must be kept up to date and fit for purpose to be effective.

---

[1] 'Business Continuity and Supply Chain Management'.

The key objectives of an effective BCM strategy should be to:

■ ensure the safety of staff;
■ maximise the defence of the organisation's reputation and brand image;
■ minimise the impact of business continuity events (including crises) on customers/clients;
■ limit/prevent impact beyond the organisation;
■ demonstrate effective and efficient governance to the media, markets and stakeholders;
■ protect the organisation's assets; and
■ meet insurance, legal and regulatory requirements.

However, BCM is not only about disaster recovery. It should be a business-owned and driven process that unifies a broad spectrum of management disciplines (see Figure 6.1.1). In particular, it is not just about IT disaster recovery. Too many organisations tend to focus all their efforts on IT because of its mission-critical nature, leaving themselves exposed on many other fronts.

Because of its all-embracing nature, the way BCM is carried out will inevitably be dependent upon, and must reflect, the nature, scale and complexity of an organisation's risk profile, risk appetite and the environment in which it operates. Inevitably, too, BCM has close links to risk management and corporate governance strategies. The importance of a holistic approach across these areas was reinforced in the Turnbull Report (1998).

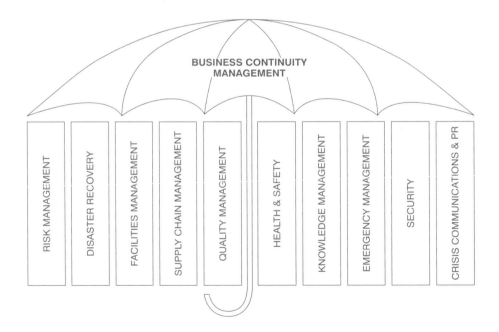

Figure 6.1.1 The unifying process – business continuity management

As an organisation can never be fully in control of its business environment, it is safe to assume that all organisations will face a business continuity event at some point. Although this simple reality has been etched in high-profile names such as Bhopal, Piper-Alpha, Perrier, Barings Bank, Challenger, Herald of Free Enterprise, Coca Cola, Exxon-Valdez, Railtrack, Canary Wharf, Enron, Anderson, Marconi, Landrover and the World Trade Centre, experience also teaches that it is the less dramatic but more frequent business continuity events that can be even more problematic to deal with. Unfortunately, it seems that many public and private organisations still think 'it will not happen to us'.

Changing the corporate culture

Ignoring business continuity issues can happen for a number of reasons, ranging from denial through disavowal to rationalisation. A process of 'group think' can develop, whereby an organisation genuinely starts to believe that their size, or some other feature, makes them immune to disaster. Or executives may firmly believe that insurance will cover them, without realising that insurance cannot indemnify against lost market share, loss of reputation or tarnished brands.

Research shows that crisis-prone organisations tend to exhibit these tendencies seven times more often than crisis-prepared organisations. Whilst all individuals may make use of such defence mechanisms from time to time, the key difference is the degree, extent and frequency with which they are used.

Changing such mindsets is not easy, and blindly implementing so-called 'best practice' business continuity techniques is not the best approach. As all organisations are different, techniques that work in one organisation will not necessarily work in another. Most executives tasked with addressing business continuity issues are keen to achieve quick wins, and the 'tick box' audit approach, which tries to copy successful strategies used elsewhere, is often adopted without consideration as to suitability.

Underlying the 'tick box' approach is the persuasive belief that a structure, policy, framework and plan is all that is required. Whilst these are critical enablers, relying on structure alone tends to overlook the key issue – that it is people who actually deal with business continuity and crises.

In this context, it is worth remembering (and reminding all senior executives) that 'managerial ignorance' is no longer an acceptable legal or moral defence if a crisis is handled badly. All managers should consider the following key questions that are likely to be asked in a subsequent inquiry:

■ When did you know there was a problem?
■ What did you do about it?
■ If you didn't do anything, why not?
■ If you didn't know there was a problem, why not?
■ What would you have done if you had known such a problem could exist?

Avoiding planning bureaucracy

There is no doubt that some sort of business continuity plan is essential. The plan becomes a source of reference at the time of a business continuity event or crisis, and the blueprint upon which the strategy and tactics of dealing with the event/crisis are designed. In particular, it can provide essential guidance on damage limitation in those short windows of opportunity that often occur at the beginning of a crisis.

Unfortunately, reputations and trust that have been built up over decades can be destroyed within minutes unless vigorously defended at a time when the speed and scale of events can overwhelm the normal operational and management systems.

A further and critical reason for having a planning process is so that the individuals who are required to implement the plan can rehearse and test what they might do in different situations. Scenario planning exercises are a very helpful technique for destruct-testing different strategies and plans.

Having said this, it is simply not possible to plan for every eventuality, and if you try to, there is a great danger of creating 'emergency' manuals that are simply too heavy to lift. A trade-off needs to be achieved between creating an effective fit-for-purpose capability and relying on untrained and untried individuals and hoping they will cope in an emergency.

The spanning of the gap between the plan and those who carry it out can be achieved by either formal tuition and/or simulations. The well-known maxim that a team is only as strong as its weakest link is worth remembering here.

The exercising of plans, rehearsing of team members and testing of solutions, systems and facilities are the elements that provide and prove an effective and fit-for-purpose capability. However, simulations are not easy to devise, and because of this, many organisations do not venture beyond the development of a plan. They are, nevertheless the best way to avoid planning bureaucracy.

Using good practice guidelines – a different approach

Because of the caveats listed earlier, the BCI's 'Business Continuity Management Good Practice Guidelines' are not intended to be a restrictive, exhaustive or definitive process to cover every eventuality within BCM. Instead, they set out to establish the generic process, principles and terminology; describe the activities and outcomes involved; and provide evaluation techniques and criteria.

These guidelines draw together the collective experience, knowledge and expertise of many leading professional members and fellows of the BCI and other authoritative professional organisations. In particular, the guidelines reflect the following BCM principles:

■ BCM and crisis management are an integral part of corporate governance;
■ BCM activities must match, focus upon and directly support the business strategy and goals of the organisation;
■ BCM must provide organisational resilience to optimise product and service availability;
■ As a value based management process, BCM must optimise cost efficiencies;
■ BCM is a business management process that is undertaken because it adds value rather than because of governance or regulatory considerations;
■ The component parts of an organisation own their business risk;
■ The management of the business risk is based upon their individual and aggregated organisational risk appetite;

- The organisation and its component parts must be accountable and responsible for maintaining an effective, up-to-date and fit-for-purpose BCM competence and capability;
- All BCM strategies, plans and solutions must be business-owned and driven;
- All BCM strategies, plans and solutions must be based upon the business mission-critical activities, their dependencies and single points of failure identified by a business impact analysis;
- All business impact analysis must be conducted in respect of business products and services in an end-to-end production context;
- There must be an agreed and published organisation policy, strategy, framework and exercising guidelines for BCM and crisis management;
- The organisation and its component parts must implement and maintain a robust exercising, rehearsal and testing programme to ensure that the business continuity capability is effective, up-to-date and fit-for-purpose;
- The relevant legal and regulatory requirements for BCM must be clearly defined and understood before undertaking a BCM programme;
- The organisation and its component parts must recognise and acknowledge that reputation, brand image, market share and shareholder value risk cannot be transferred or removed by internal sourcing and/or outsourcing;
- BCM implications must be considered at all stages of the development of new business operations, products, services and organisational infrastructure projects;
- BCM implications must be considered as an essential part of the business change management process;
- The competency of BCM practitioners should be based and benchmarked against the 10 professional competency standards of the BCI;
- All third parties, including joint venture companies and service providers, upon whom an organisation is critically dependent for the provision of products, services, support or data, must be required to demonstrate an effective, proven and fit-for-purpose BCM capability;
- The standard terms and conditions of any outsourced and/or internal sourcing of products, services, support or data should reflect these good practice guidelines.

The structure and format of the guidelines is based upon the most frequently asked questions in relation to BCM, which are listed in Figure 6.1.2.

Guideline component heading	Most frequently asked questions
PURPOSE	■ Why do we need it?
OUTCOMES	■ What will it achieve?
COMPONENTS	■ What do we need to do to it? ■ What does it consist of (ingredients)?
METHODOLOGIES & TECHNIQUES	■ What are the tools to do it?
PROCESS	■ How is it done? ■ How do we do it?
FREQUENCY & TRIGGERS	■ When should it be done?
PARTICIPANTS	■ Who does it? ■ Who should be involved?
DELIVERABLES	■ What is the output?
'GOOD PRACTICE' EVALUATION CRITERIA	■ How do we know if we have got it right?

Figure 6.1.2 BCM questions

The BCM life-cycle

The BCI principles and frequently asked questions have been drawn together to create the BCM life-cycle (see Figure 6.1.3), an interactive process tool to guide the implementation of an effective BCM process. The six stages of the life-cycle are set out in more detail in Figure 6.1.4.

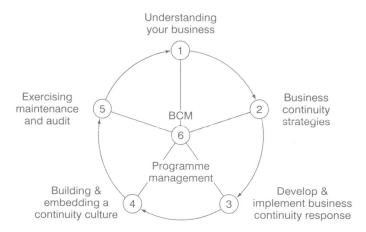

Figure 6.1.3 The business continuity life-cycle

The guidelines have been used to generate a tool for evaluating the BCM process, which takes the form of a spreadsheet current state assessment (benchmark) workbook (see Figure 6.1.5). The workbook enables and facilitates good practice compliance evaluation, current state assessment gap analysis, assurance and benchmarking (process and performance).

Each organisation needs to assess how to apply the 'good practice', contained within the guidelines, to their own organisation. They must ensure that their BCM competence and capability meets the nature, scale and complexity of their business, and reflects their individual culture and operating environment.

1. UNDERSTANDING YOUR BUSINESS	■ Business impact analysis ■ Risk assessment and control
2. BCM STRATEGIES	■ Organisation (corporate) BCM strategy ■ Process level BCM strategy ■ Resource recovery BCM strategy
3. DEVELOPING & IMPLENTING A BCM RESPONSE	■ Plans and planning ■ External bodies and organisations ■ Crisis/BCM event/incident management ■ Sourcing (intra-organisation and/or outsourcing providers) ■ Emergency response and operations ■ Communications ■ Public relations and PR
4. BUILDING & EMBEDDING A BCM CULTURE	■ An ongoing programme of education, awareness and training
5. EXERCISING, MAINTENANCE & AUDIT	■ Exercising of BCM plans ■ Rehearsal of staff, BCM teams ■ Testing of technology and BCM systems ■ BCM maintenance ■ BCM audit
6. THE BCM PROGRAMME	■ Board commitment and proactive participation ■ Organisation (corporate) BCM strategy ■ BCM policy ■ BCM framework ■ Roles, accountability, responsibility and authority ■ Finance ■ Resources ■ Assurance ■ Audit ■ Management information system (MIS): metrics/scorecard/benchmark ■ Compliance: legal/regulatory issues ■ Change management

Figure 6.1.4 The six stages of the life-cycle in more detail

STAGE 1: **UNDERSTANDING YOUR** **BUSINESS** Organisation strategy Operational and business objectives	Critical business factors (mission critical activities)	Business outputs and deliverables (services and products)	**Maturity** **Level** 1
STAGE 2: **BUSINESS CONTINUITY** **MANAGEMENT STRATEGIES** Organisation (corporate) BCM strategy	Process level BCM strategy	Resource recovery BCM strategy	2
STAGE 3: **BUSINESS CONTINUITY** **SOLUTIONS AND PLANS** Business continuity plans	Resource recovery solutions and plans	Crisis management plan	3
STAGE 4: **BUILDING AND EMBEDDING A** **BCM CULTURE** BCM culture and awareness programme	Education and culture building activities	BCM training programme	4
STAGE 5: **EXERCISING, MAINTENANCE** **AND AUDIT OF BCM** Exercising of BCM	Maintenance of BCM	Audit of BCM	5
STAGE 6: **BCM PROGRAMME** **MANAGEMENT**	BCM policy	BCM assurance	6

Figure 6.1.5 The BCM process

Crisis management

The key elements of a crisis management framework are slightly different to the BCM life-cycle, and include those set out in Figure 6.1.6, but the list should not be seen as restrictive or exhaustive. There are many advantages to adopting a modular approach to a crisis or business continuity situation, not least that it can be easily and quickly modified to suit local, national as well as global requirements.

However, in managing any event it is critical to recognise that a successful outcome is judged by both the technical response, and the perceived competence and capability of the management in delivering the business response. The stakeholder perception should be seen as the critical success factor with an equal, if not more urgent, priority over the technical solution. Consequently, the acid test is to convincingly demonstrate an effective and fit-for-purpose business continuity and crisis management capability, and to continue business as usual. This is in contrast to the more familiar pattern of a fall and recovery of a business, which is more representative of the outdated disaster recovery and business resumption approaches.

BUSINESS RISK CONTROL
■ Monitoring
■ Prevention
■ Planning and preparation
■ Crisis identification
ASSESSMENT
■ Crisis evaluation (including evaluation criteria)
INVOCATION AND ESCALATION
MANAGEMENT AND RECOVERY
CLOSURE AND REVIEW
■ Formal closure
■ Ongoing issues eg investigation and litigation
■ Post-crisis review and report
IMPROVEMENT
■ Implementation of approved post-crisis review report recommendations

Figure 6.1.6 Crisis management

Conclusions

An organisation consists of people, and people at the top who give a cultural lead. As a consequence, business continuity and crisis management are not solely a set of tools, techniques and mechanisms to be implemented in an organisation. They should reflect a more general mood, attitude and type of action taken by managers and staff. Individual personalities play a crucial and critical role. It is the human factor that is frequently underestimated in BCM. This is of particular importance because the examination of the cause of business continuity events and crises usually identifies several warning signals that were ignored or not recognised. The key to a successful crisis and BCM capability is to adopt an holistic approach to validate each of the key building blocks of the process.

The first task is always to identify the right people who are not bound as individuals or within the corporate culture. It is on these criteria that the success or failure of creating an effective and fit-for-purpose BCM capability will be determined. Having identified the right people, they should engage in the BCM planning process using the BCI Good Practice Guidelines and training via the exercise simulations of plans, rehearsal of people/teams and testing of systems, processes, technology, structures and communications.

The organisation can assist this process by appointing a BCM 'champion' at a senior level whose role is to draw together, under a matrix team approach, representatives from the various organisation functions (eg human resources), together with a key line of business heads to ensure a co-ordinated approach. The key advantage of this approach is that it builds on what already exists and has been done, thereby enabling a 'virtual capability' that provides cost efficiency. A further benefit is that it ensures 'buy-in' throughout the organisation.

In adopting this methodology and regularly exercising, rehearsing and testing, the organisation maintains an effective up-to-date and fit-for-purpose BCM and crisis management capability. When a crisis hits the organisation everyone knows what to do and a smooth invocation of the plan takes place ensuring that the impact on mission critical activities is minimal.

This article first appeared in the *Quartile Review* published in January 2003 by the Faculty of Finance and Management of the Institute of Accountant's of England and Wales.

Dr David Smith FBCI is Chair of the BCI Education Committee, member of the BCI Board and editor of the BCI Good Practice Guide to Business Continuity Management. The Business Continuity Institute's mission is to promote the art and science of Business Continuity Management worldwide.

The BCI promotes the highest standards of professional competence and commercial ethics in the provision, maintenance and services for Business Continuity Management (BCM). It provides an internationally recognised certification scheme for BCM managers and practitioners. The BCI Professional Recognition Programme creates a benchmark for the assessment of best practice in the field.

There are now over 1250 members of the Institute working in 40 countries across the world. Members are drawn from all sectors including Finance, Government, Health, Transport, Retail and Manufacturing. The BCI is currently working with the FSA and UK Cabinet Office on good practice guides for BCM.

For further information contact the Institute on Tel: +44 (0)870 603 8783; Email: TheBCI@btinternet.com; Website: www.thebci.org

Data recovery

Don't dice with your data, says Gordon Stevenson, Managing Director of Vogon International, and don't panic in an emergency.

If people are a company's most valuable asset, then data comes a close second. As companies become more dependent on technology for all aspects of their operations, the information contained on computer disks and back-up tapes can mean the difference between continued success and failure. While most companies believe that their data is safe, many may not have set up even the most basic of back-up systems to protect it and data loss can happen to anyone.

How does data loss happen?

Although data is a valuable commodity, not enough emphasis is placed on protecting this vulnerable asset from loss. While computer hardware and software are fallible, humans are notoriously even more so. Unfortunately many companies and individuals do not have – or do not put into practice – adequate back-up procedures, leaving themselves open to data loss. The majority of problems are caused by human error, such as accidentally overwriting back-up tapes, deleting important files, inadvertently formatting a hard disk or mishandling a laptop.

Malicious data loss can also be an issue, particularly where companies fail to make appropriate use of passwords. While there needs to be a balance between the complexity and frequency of password change and the ease with which users can remember them, to have passwords – even at the basic user level – that are common knowledge makes a company unnecessarily vulnerable. It is not unusual to find a list of everyone's password stored in an easily accessible place within an office, or even a board displaying 'this week's password'.

Even if your staff are competent and trustworthy, hardware and software can still fail unexpectedly. Operating systems or packages may contain bugs or become corrupt, causing them to malfunction, with consequences such as overwritten data. Power surges from the power supply, or lightning, can also cause damage to computer equipment, and it is possible for the motor or the control board of a hard disk to burn out, locking its data inside, or for the disk just to fail. When disaster strikes on a larger scale, there is always the more dramatic risk of fire and water damage too.

Do nothing

Unfortunately, many companies are not prepared for the reality of hard disk or tape failure and often make a bad situation much worse. Retrievable data is often lost through inappropriate attempts to recover it.

Simply rebooting a computer can cause the data to be overwritten permanently, as the system creates temporary files in supposedly unused space. A physically damaged disk can become significantly more damaged, sometimes to the point of no data being recoverable.

If a disk has ceased to function, the worst possible course of action is to attempt a DIY repair. To recover their contents, broken hard disks should be opened up in a laboratory environment using special tools and techniques. Even disturbing the screws on the casing of a drive can destroy critical alignments, making reading the data impossible, or perhaps causing the drive to crash if subsequently run.

Therefore, when vital data has been lost, the most important first step is to leave everything alone.

Calling in the experts

Whilst commercial data recovery tools exist, their use is not advisable as it is highly unlikely that a software tool written months ago, perhaps a continent away, can accurately diagnose the difference between a corrupted file system and a damaged head. These tools always provide a 'best guess' at what the problem is, and then give you the option to 'go ahead and write to the media', which is not a particularly safe thing to do. Sometimes it is necessary to write customised programs for individual recoveries. When data has been lost because of software corruption rather than physical damage, extracting and rebuilding the files is the major process in recovery.

Data recovery experts, such as Vogon International, do not work directly on the damaged medium itself but use a technique called 'imaging' to create an exact copy of the entire contents of a disk. This allows data to be manipulated and restructured independently of its source, and recovered data can be returned on whatever medium is requested.

Tapes are a sequential storage medium and, as such, present their own specialist recovery problems. If a problem occurs at any point along the tape, this can prevent access to data beyond the damage. Recording errors can occur and tapes can also be accidentally overwritten in a way that effectively blocks the ability to read the surviving data. Tapes are also susceptible to snapping, crumpling and extremes of temperature.

Protecting yourself

'Don't panic' is the first piece of advice to remember in a data loss emergency, and 'do nothing' – except call the experts – is the second. However, there are a number of simple steps you can take to protect your company against disaster.

■ Put in place a regular, reliable back-up regime and make sure that it is strictly implemented by trained personnel. This should include a verification process to make sure that the back-ups work and are recording the correct files.
■ Duplicate the back-up to a second type of media so that if one fails the other is available.
■ Monitor the back-up to ensure that it has taken place and watch out for signs of anything unusual in the way the system operates. Record on hard copy the results of back-ups to help make this comparison.
■ Keep at least one set of back-up tapes off site so that, if your premises burn down or are flooded, you will not lose your data. This is standard business continuity best practice and easy to implement.
■ Back up before installing any new software. This may be a chore but it is essential!
■ If possible, leave your systems on all the time in consistent environmental conditions – hardware failure happens most often at start-up and shut-down.
■ Keep up with technology. Back-up tapes that can only be read with a drive that hasn't been manufactured since 1989 will be inaccessible when the elderly device breaks down.

Computers are not infallible and any piece of hardware will eventually fail. No company would fail to protect its business premises by not installing smoke detectors, burglar alarms and fire extinguishers, or by leaving its doors unlocked overnight. Protecting data, and knowing what to do in the event of an emergency, should be as much a priority for all organisations.

Vogon International has rapidly become a global leader in data recovery from all types of computer storage media, as well as data conversion and computer investigation. Its client base ranges from commercial business to law enforcement agencies and tax authorities throughout the EU, Asia and North America. With over 17 years' experience, Vogon operates worldwide from its base in Oxfordshire, England. Vogon GmbH is based in Munich, Germany, and Vogon LLC is based in Oklahoma, USA; both are wholly-owned subsidiaries of Vogon International.

For further information contact: Sandie Stevenson. Tel: +44 (0)1869 355 255, or see the website at www.vogon-international.com

Crisis management

Disasters are usually a result of organisations failing to prevent a crisis from getting worse, says Peter Power, Managing Director at Visor Consultants Limited.

'There cannot be a crisis next week. My schedule is already full', said Henry Kissinger in June 1969 at a time when the US faced many potential crises. Humorous yes, but is there some truth in what he said? How many potential disasters are already on your corporate radar screen that you are too busy to notice?

There you are, convinced that you have planned for just about everything. Your risk analysis is complete and all your information and data processing seems watertight. You are confident that you are as prepared as you can be for most eventualities. Even the chairman has shown an interest. But what if fate delivers you a low ball and you have a crisis that really is out of the blue? How would you cope?

There is a worrying tendency, especially in the US, that assumes any 'out of the blue' crisis means just that: aircraft leaving the sky and deliberately hitting tall buildings – and we have all seen many post-9/11 business continuity plans that now focus exclusively on this threat to the exclusion of all others.

Whilst it is true that our notion of terrorism as a form of limited violence was shattered by the terrible events in 2001, previous attacks by equally less predictable terrorist organisations – like the Aum sect in Japan, responsible for the Tokyo subway nerve gas attack and fanatical groups in the Middle East – had already challenged our previous assumptions about terrorism. It was, and will always be, a threat that is surprisingly hard to define. Almost by definition, terrorism will continually seek to change its face. But enough has already been written on this subject and before we also slide towards overindulging our concern with just one type of threat, let us return to the subject of this chapter: can you really handle any crisis?

In March 2000, a lightening bolt caused a blaze at a Philips electronic factory in Albuquerque in the United States. Ten minutes later the fire was out, but far away in Scandinavia this small event sparked a corporate crisis that shifted the balance of power between two of Europe's largest electronics companies.

Nokia and Ericsson both depended on computer chips from the Philips factory. Indeed, the supply was critical to each company. After the fire Philips needed weeks to return to normal capacity, but with mobile phone sales booming, neither company in Scandinavia could afford to wait. What happened next is a lesson for us all.

Nokia (Europe's largest corporation by market capitalisation) immediately switched on their crisis management skills. Before Philips said anything, all they noticed was a glitch in the flow of chips – but it was on their radar screen. Within a few days they had scoured Europe for alternate suppliers, flexed the company muscle to squeeze more out of them and patched together a solution that ensured manufacture of handsets kept going. Pertti Korhonen, the chief trouble-shooter for Nokia, said afterwards. 'A crisis is the moment when you improvise.' He was correct.

Ericsson, on the other hand, were probably too busy to notice anything. By the time it was realised that their supply of chips from Albuquerque was in jeopardy it was too late. Nokia had been there days before and taken all that was left, and had done the same with most other suppliers. In the end, Ericsson lost around US$600 million of revenue and 50 per cent of market share and subsequently had to be rescued by linking with Sony to sell any handsets.

In my experience, the majority of disasters are caused by organisations that fail to prevent a crisis from getting worse, and then only wake up when things have deteriorated to the point of disaster. My own belief is that crisis prevention is considerably more effective than disaster recovery, but many organisations are encouraged by some consultants to spend a disproportionate amount of time and money on recovery options, without first looking at reducing risks, as well as preparing for the unforeseen. So what are the drivers for crisis management? Here are a few:

■ protection of reputation and brand;
■ customer service;
■ shareholder value;
■ legislation, regulation and corporate governance;
■ increased complexity of business operations;
■ increased interdependencies;
■ insurance conditions.

The last point, about insurance, also includes a potential reduction in premium if you can demonstrate that, should a catastrophe appear, being able to work at the speed of a crisis rather than at the speed of the organisation, the likelihood of a subsequent claim on your policy is much reduced. It is also worth bearing in mind that most insurers accept that for every pound or dollar of insured costs, there is anything between 8 and 36 times this amount in uninsured costs. Typically these costs are:

■ management time;
■ investigation costs;
■ adverse publicity;

- loss of reputation;
- loss of brand;
- loss of image;
- fines and penalties;
- loss of expertise.

But realising this is not enough. It is also important to know that stakeholders and customers will now want to measure board proposals on issues such as succession, accounting irregularities, fraud and resilience. In 2003, as global threats and risks become more diverse and worrying, we might assume that being able to work instantly as crisis managers links more to profit than to cost. Nokia thought so. It follows that none of this should be seen as a 'grudge purchase' but as an extension of sound corporate governance executive stewardship – especially in a post-Enron/Worldcom world. So how do you do it?

Over the years we have helped many organisations in the UK, US and Europe to create, train and test their own 'crisis teams' and have realised that there are a few important points that should always be borne in mind:

- When you are analysing data and researching the best options on how to prepare, always remember to 'keep your eye on the ball' and not let the project get hijacked by something else. All the plans, mission statements, recovery options and supply chain goodwill counts for nothing if executives cannot switch to 'quick time' thinking and form a 'crisis management cell' without delay. It is, therefore, a subject where selection, coaching, testing and exercising counts for everything.
- Your own suppliers may cause you to have a crisis. These days many companies operate 'just-in-time' (JIT) procedures, which probably means they cannot deal with 'just-in-case' events since there is little or no slack left in the process. Add to that fragile supply and data routes up- and down-stream from your sites and the knock-on effect of someone else's crisis seems all too obvious.
- Getting board-level agreement is not enough. You must get board-level commitment and hands-on involvement.
- Make sure that crisis management becomes a truly operational tool and not just a reference whose purpose is to reassure everyone when things are calm. It must be an integral part of management and a continuous process, of which the document marked 'plan' is simply a written presentation of management competence.
- Avoid lack of motivation and inspiration. What do I mean by this? Well, take the story of an important visitor who some years ago called into a stone quarry to see what the workers were up to. All around him apprentices were busy chipping at granite blocks. 'What are you doing?' he asked one of them. 'I'm making a stone block that will be two feet long by a foot wide', came the answer. Turning to another apprentice he asked the same question but got a different answer: 'Oh, I'm part of the team building a magnificent cathedral'.
- Manage your risks properly and recognise that the key to successful crisis management is to realise that containing a crisis is more effective than recovering from a disaster. Oddly enough, many organisations have disaster recovery plans, but not enough have crisis management options. Perhaps that is because you can more easily measure recovery? This leads to the last point:

■ When setting up any measurement criteria, seek out what is important and then work out how to measure it (for example, measuring the likely damage to reputation). At the beginning of the Vietnam War, the US Army had numerous fire-fights with the Vietnamese Army and quickly realised that the number of enemy dead invariably far exceeded their own. This was easy to measure and thus could be used to calculate who would win the war, and how soon. However, in doing this the US Army, like many before it, made the mistake of finding something to measure and then making it important, rather than the other way around. For the Vietnamese Army, leaving the dead in the field was irrelevant when you had endless reserves, control over domestic media coverage and a will to win.

The truth is that almost all crises follow a path from normality to possible disaster. Crisis management can recognise and interrupt this if applied diligently and on time. In the case of a bomb explosion without warning, this path will be sudden; but such a scenario is an exception, as many incidents can be termed 'quiet catastrophes' that build up, often unnoticed (small errors that are not checked soon become big problems). This can include scenarios such as power failure, intermittent system faults, road closures, sabotage, protestors, corrupt data, or building-related issues such as faulty air conditioning.

Sometimes organisations have first been alerted to a crisis because the press called to tell them – in which case they might already be halfway down the path to disaster where trying to take the 'media high ground' is even more imperative. Indeed, the issue of presentation and media image is so important that we have seen some companies ultimately fail even though their efforts on site were as good as they could be, but they somehow failed to give the right message to the world's media. When speaking to the press, try and avoid the five 'd's:

■ denying everything;
■ doing nothing;
■ diverting to someone else;
■ diminishing the incident;
■ drip-feeding at your own pace.

It is often the case that organisations have not necessarily taken the wrong actions in terms of crisis management but probably took the right ones too late – by which time the crisis itself sets the pace and you might end up following events rather than getting in front and stopping the spread.

By calculating an assessment of the crisis situation and its likely development – coupled with what should be the ideal reaction to control, contain and resolve it – it is possible to draw a basic model to illustrate the point that few crises instantly jump from normality to disaster.

It is therefore possible to assess the impact of the crisis and its likely rise/fall, and then link this directly to the best reaction to contain it, to reassure stakeholders, and so on. In this way a crisis management structure can quickly be set up, but populated only according to present and anticipated requirements. For example, there is a 'stage 1' crisis that puts some people on standby whilst others are engaged in 'fire fighting'. Subsequently, the incident can be either downgraded or upgraded to a 'stage 2' crisis, where levels may be fully staffed on a shift basis. The outline structure, however, remains the same.

But setting all this out in a few pages may ignore a particularly vital feature. Unfortunately, too many crisis planners often overlook human emotion. Too many practitioners see the processes they are dealing with as highly systematic, cerebral and conscious: you know what you are doing and you can explain the process to others. Emotion is seen as something that clutters up the calm processing of information and is nearly always factored out of the equation. That is one reason why my own company specialises in crisis management, since when your own schedule is full and human emotion is ignored you can be sure that a crisis is soon to follow.

Peter Power is MD of Visor Consultants Limited. He was the lead speaker at 2002 Global Disaster Management conference in North America and is a Special Advisor to the Canadian Centre for Emergency Preparedness, as well as the UK Disaster Management Forum. Peter also wrote the UK Government-issued guidebook *Preventing Chaos in a Crisis* and led many front-line crisis teams at several terrorist and other major events in London while a senior police officer at New Scotland Yard. He regularly lectures on his experiences and occasionally speaks on BBC TV/radio. He is a Fellow of the Institute of Management, Fellow of the Business Continuity Institute, and a member of the Institute of Risk Management.

For further information contact: Peter Power, MD, Visor Consultants Limited, 212 Piccadilly, London W1J 9HG. Tel: +44 (0)20 7917 6026; Fax: +44 (0)20 7439 0262; Mobile Tel: +44 (0)7774 824487; Email: info@visorconsultants.com; Website: www.visorconsultants.com

Forensics

A computer forensics investigation can reveal practically everything about the perpetrator of a crime, says Clifford May, Principal Consultant at Integralis, but you must know where to look – and not destroy any evidence.

Chains of evidence

Contrary to popular perception, most e-business and information security crimes and abuses that are reported today are internally inspired and range from theft of information to sabotage. As a result, the work of the *computer forensics* expert is a far more complex operation than most people appreciate.

Computer forensics enables the systematic and careful identification of evidence in computer-related crime and abuse cases. This may range from tracing the tracks of a hacker through an organisation's IT systems, to tracing the originator of apparently anonymous defamatory emails, to recovering evidence of fraud. But, as with any investigation, it is vital to know where to look to find the evidence required and how not to destroy that very evidence in the process. This requires skill, knowledge and a lot of experience – especially as all forensic investigations must respect the laws governing the rights of the individual in each country and must always be handled with sensitivity.

A computer forensics investigation can reveal practically everything, from the character of the user, to their interests, activities, financial health, acquaintances and more. It is all there to be recovered from applications, email systems, Internet browsers and free space. Their life, outlook, intelligence and interactions are held – as individual as any fingerprint – on the computer they use. There is no limit to the accountability that can be uncovered: private business transactions, communications with accomplices, fraud indicators and much more are frequently mined from systems. Attempts to hide or erase this evidence are often unsuccessful, and a 'golden nugget' that proves a crime can be unearthed by an expert.

The evidence that a forensics investigation will seek to uncover will vary; but activity such as Internet abuse during working hours is a good example of a well-known business problem. Amongst the more prevalent cases tend to be problems involving employees who divulge critical corporate information to third parties, fraud and the diversion of sales to rival companies for generous kickbacks. Cases of anonymous harassment and defamation are increasing along with the use of email and the Internet, and hacking cases involving Trojan horses, denial of service attacks and network intrusions also feature highly in the typical forensics workload.

Industrial espionage is also still a problem, and the discovery of 'key loggers' is increasing with improved user awareness. A small hardware device or software utility such as this can easily be installed and go unnoticed. These simple tools can help a competitor or criminal to steal passwords and user IDs in an instant. Without the correct security procedures, the victim won't know a thing about it until it's too late.

But it is not only employees that forensics investigations focus on. So few companies have adequate security vetting procedures, that industrial espionage has become a global concern. Every computer, on practically every desk, is an open doorway to the company's network and all of its data and essential information, such as its payroll, projects, R&D, finance, patents and customer details. Everything is potentially there for the taking by professionals posing as cleaners, tradesmen, maintenance crews, fitters and even, sometimes, as clients.

Cases of arson have been brought to trial using computer forensic techniques, and bandwidth problems in large corporations have been found to be a result of network abuse by personnel downloading massive video files (sometimes full-length, hi-resolution feature films), MP3 music files, or simply spending all day listening to global radio over the Internet. Petty jealousy is also an increasing problem in many organisations: better cars, larger offices, fatter salaries and unpopular promotions can provoke the worst kind of unreasonable behaviour. The result is that sabotage is a growing problem, with people systematically and knowingly breaking systems.

Gathering the evidence

The process of gathering evidence requires proper incident management training. Investigators must follow the correct procedures or the evidence may be compromised and become inadmissible. Simply booting a PC will change at least 70 of its parameters. In addition, documentation of the steps taken in a forensic investigation is vital, and a case can be built on suspicious activity. Why does the suspect work so often at weekends? Why does he/she never take leave? Is there a regular pattern of people who always work long hours, often late into the evening? The ideal is to take copies of the entire hard drives of the suspect systems for examination with forensic software, but this is not always possible and a strict procedure for identifying and securing potential evidence is required.

There is also an array of pitfalls to be avoided when attempting to secure reliable evidence: it must not be damaged, destroyed or compromised in any way, and steps must be taken to ensure that the investigation:

■ does not change any of the time and date stamps of files;
■ does not change the contents of the data itself;

- maintains a complete and comprehensive audit trail of the steps taken;
- understands what operations the computer performs when it is turned on or off.

Computer forensics is a growing area that is earning increasingly wider recognition; and as systems and networks increase in complexity, it is becoming more and more specialised. It is also the area for specialist companies who have the resources, knowledge and experience to really make a difference. There is a growing awareness of the requirements for handling computer evidence in the UK due to an established and accepted code of practice and the number of cases passing through the Courts. However, the chain of evidence is frequently not confined to one country and may cover many different countries and several continents, requiring forensic specialists to understand international law.

It is also important to remember that it is only possible to uncover what is actually there. This may seem like an obvious point to make, but computer forensics cannot promise or perform miracles, and the most obvious pieces of evidence, such as a letter written to an accomplice, logging dates, times and transactions, found in the free space on a disk is a highly unusual occurrence.

A really good forensics team can tell, in an instant, whether a business has good grounds for further investigation or not. They will know from their initial examination whether something looks wrong and out of place. Such a decision can often save a company many thousands of pounds and a lot of wasted time.

As the discipline develops, forensics is spreading into whole new areas. Specialist teams are not only being tasked with handling criminal incidents but also with developing and implementing blocking, prevention and tracking techniques in companies and throughout organisations. But the fact is that most hacking cases are not pursued as far as they should be – companies simply rebuild their systems and get on with business, due to fear of the expense and loss of time that prosecution might involve. Forensic specialists are increasingly advising on the viability of potential courses of action, and are increasingly being called upon to help pinpoint sources of danger and devise procedures that prevent repeat attacks.

Theft of company information and intellectual property is still the largest area of corporate crime, and computer forensics is certain to grow in importance as the volume of e-commerce transactions increases and as access to company networks and corporate information needs to be more reliably protected and ever-more tightly controlled.

Integralis, the corporate solutions division of Articon-Integralis, provides information security solutions to all industry sectors throughout the world, allowing organisations to grow and achieve their business goals securely. These solutions combine service and system integration, the deployment of 'best-of-breed' security products and managed security services, and employ some of the leading technologists and most skilled engineers in the industry.

Integralis is recognised as a leading and trusted provider of information security solutions in the European IT and e-commerce security market.

For further information contact: Integralis Ltd, Theale House, Brunel Road, Theale, Reading RG7 4AQ. Tel: +44 (0)118 930 6060; Fax +44 (0)118 930 2143; Email: info@integralis.co.uk; Website: www.integralis.co.uk

Index of advertisers

BSI Management Systems	v
Centrinet	90–91
ClearCommerce	78
Computacenter	xvii
Indicii Salus	ii
INSL	164
Integralis	2
Macrovision	88
NetScreen	ix
Nokia	xi
NTA Monitor	124
Positive Internet	vi
Proseq	xii
Tekdata	52